THE QUEST

A Lifelong Journey in Spiritual Growth

by Lois Brown Shipman

WINEPRESS WP PUBLISHING

Printed in the United States of America.

Packaged by WinePress Publishing, PO Box 428, Enumclaw, WA 98022. The views expressed or implied in this work do not necessarily reflect those of WinePress Publishing. Ultimate design, content, and editorial accuracy of this work are the responsibilities of the author.

ISBN 1-57921-381-2
Library of Congress Catalog Card Number: 2001088904

This book is dedicated to Timothy and Jay Carl, two children from the inner city of Washington, D.C., in memory of our happy times together before their lives ended prematurely.

Contents

Preface

This book is a life story, but I do not consider myself to be the central character. I would never have written a book as a memoir of my life. That it is about my life experiences is evident from the chapter titles. However, these experiences are only background for the true theme, which is the story of my spiritual growth as I struggled for meaning in my life and the strength to meet new and challenging experiences confronting me.

Two wars—World War II and the Korean War—lifted me from a small town in Minnesota to a life of international travel and overseas living. My husband's later work with the World Bank led to a life in Washington, D.C., that included two trips around the world. Against this backdrop of travel and wars, including an evacuation from Egypt by the U.S. Navy during the Suez Invasion of 1956, I came to know Jesus Christ and grow in Him. In this lifelong Quest, I sought and found my Savior, Jesus Christ of Nazareth.

As with any book, this one would not have been possible without the inspiration and help of many others. First of all, I'd like to acknowledge Susan Dunlop, M.B.A., of the Minnesota Medical Foundation at the University of Minnesota, who first gave me the idea and encouragement to put my story on paper. I'd also like to recognize my younger son, Richard, for his work with the physical preparation of the manuscript and use of his photo for the cover design (taken at the Upper Falls of Yellowstone National Park). Finally, thanks to Laura Slough for the beautiful and original cover design and to the librarians of Bill Memorial Library for their gracious tolerance as I copied this story longhand day by day in their charming surroundings!

Lois Brown Shipman
January 2001

Part One: The Quest Begins

1

World War II

As I look back, somehow is was very fitting that my spiritual Quest started with the birth of my first son on November 8, 1941. Due to complications, he was left in the hospital for a month, so it was December 7, 1941, when my husband and I at long last picked him up. As we were driving to our home in Minneapolis, Minnesota, we turned on the radio and heard the news that Japan had attacked Pearl Harbor. From that moment, my world was turned upside down and America was catapulted into a defining era in our country's and the world's history.

We had two years of comparative normalcy following the outbreak of war, but in 1943, my husband decided to volunteer for service with the Army. At the time, we were living in Mankato, a small town in the southern part of Minnesota. Shippy, as he was known to all, was a public health engineer and was not drafted when war was declared because his work was considered essential. Nevertheless, he felt his work in environmental health was also vital to the Army, and he wanted to serve his country in this time of crisis. As a young wife of twenty-five with a two-year-old son, I was not exactly jumping for joy, but we both were aware of the issues at stake. We also loved our country and wanted to serve, each in our own way. I knew he had to go, and I knew I must say yes. What I did *not* know was that I was to be like a leaf in a storm, lifted up by forces stronger than myself and shaped by experiences beyond my control.

To backtrack a bit, I experienced serious complications with my first pregnancy. In November, I was taken to the hospital for observation. The doctors assured my husband and parents that birth was not imminent, so my loved ones said good-bye and left. I was alone on the examination table half-listening to the consultations among the three or four doctors around me, my thoughts drifting. Imagine my shock when shortly thereafter the doctors proclaimed, "The baby must be removed *at once!*" Then there were discussions about what procedures to use. I sensed the urgency and depth of their concern.

Their concern was nothing compared to mine! Number one, I was alone (except for the doctors, of course). And number two, I was very—and I mean *very*—scared! I was sure I was going to die along with the baby. *What to do? What to do?*

I had been brought up in the church and knew about Jesus, but He was just a name to me. However, as I lay there, I decided to give my baby to Jesus. For myself, I said the Twenty-third Psalm over and over and was very thankful for my church—and for my good memory!

I did not die, as is evident from this story, nor did my baby. I took him home that fateful December day and recovered to a comparatively normal life. I say comparatively, because after all, it was wartime.

2

Mankato, Minnesota

That "comparatively normal life" was soon to end, as my husband was transferred to Brookley Air Force Base in Mobile, Alabama, early in 1944. My son and I stayed behind in Mankato. In the meantime, I discovered that I was expecting another child, with a due date in mid-September. Fortunately, my parents and extended family were in Minneapolis, so they were not too far away. Also, we were renting a charming new house in Mankato that I dearly loved. Life went on, as it does, war or no war, and I had it much better than most. I settled in for the duration of the war—or so I thought. How mistaken I was!

One problem I found irritating was an eye infection I developed early in my second pregnancy. The doctor could not find the source of the infection, so treatment was limited to a black patch over my left eye. I felt a bit glamorous and distinctive!

After my first son, Bruce, was born I had started to read my Bible. Each day I was learning how to pray. I knew I needed to know Jesus better, as I was now facing a new crisis. With Shippy away, I would be a single mother, and I needed strength, bodily and spiritually, to meet life in a positive and constructive way. I had to know more than just Jesus' name and the Twenty-third Psalm. I was a "baby Christian," but I was learning.

I especially empathized with Paul in 2 Corinthians 12:7–10:

> And lest I should be exalted above measure by the abundance of the revelations, a thorn in the flesh was given to me, a messenger of Satan to buffet me, lest I be exalted above measure. Concerning this thing I pleaded with the Lord three times that it might depart from me And He said to me, "My Grace is sufficient for you, for My strength is made perfect in weakness." Therefore most gladly I will rather boast in my infirmities, that the power of Christ may rest upon me. Therefore I take pleasure in infirmity, in reproaches, in needs, in persecutions, in distress, for Christ's sake. For when I am weak, then I am strong.

These verses were especially meaningful to me, as it is speculated that Paul's "thorn" pertained to his eyes. I wasn't quite to the point where I could "boast in my infirmities," but I memorized all the verses, and they gave me strength and encouragement. I was brought a step closer to Jesus. He was now not just a *Name* but was becoming a *Friend.*

Unexpectedly, on August 30, 1944, the baby due in mid-September decided to come early. Déjà vu! Here I was alone again. *Where to start? What to do?* I grabbed the telephone and called the doctor to see what he would advise.

"Come to the hospital *at once*!" he said. Because of the complications with my first pregnancy, he had been watching me closely.

I called a neighbor to pick up Bruce, who was now two, threw some things in a case, called a taxi, tucked my Bible under my arm, said a prayer, and was off to the hospital.

Some hours later, a 6-pound son, Richard, arrived safely. I gave thanks to God. This time I was not alone with just a *name* and the Twenty-third Psalm. At this point in my Quest,

I had a *friend* I was learning to know and the assurance of His words to Paul, “My Grace is sufficient for you for My strength is made perfect in weakness” (2 Cor. 12:9).

My Mother, when informed that the baby had already arrived was, as my Grandmother used to say, “in a state”! She arrived from Minneapolis in due time and stayed with me until we found a girl to help with the new baby. Alas, that was the first of a number of “states” my dear Mother would endure in the span of my peripatetic life. The next was not far away!

3

En Route to Mobile

In December 1944, I received the news that my husband had been ordered to the Pacific, effective in a matter of weeks. Richard was into his fourth month and Bruce had just celebrated his third birthday. Nevertheless, I decided at once to fly to Mobile with the children to say goodbye. Now this really put my parents into a "state." To be absolutely truthful, my Dad took it well, but Mother was agitated.

Mother pleaded, "Lois, you cannot get a flight to Mobile. And if you could, you'd have to change planes in Chicago. You know this is wartime and they are bumping people all the time for priority military."

"Lois, your eye is still troubling you and it is only three months since the baby was born.

"Lois, you are to be a bridesmaid in Geraldine's wedding.

"Lois, you just can't take those little ones down there."

But to all my mother's arguments I had only one reply, "I may never see my husband again.

"At least leave the children with me," she begged.

"Shippy may never see his children again."

"At least leave the baby with me."

"Shippy has never seen his new son. I must say goodbye."

Mother finally gave up.

I was able to get seats on a flight to Chicago, where I was scheduled to change planes for the flight to Mobile. The departure day came, and being Minnesota in December, it started to snow. The plane was scheduled to leave at noon, so we started early for the airport. Mother, Dad, and I, with the baby wrapped in a blanket and Bruce holding my hand, climbed into the car with our small suitcase.

In the beginning, we drove along at a normal speed, but as time passed the snow increased, and we were compelled to drive more carefully and slowly. The clock was ticking away inexorably, and I was clutching my baby tighter and tighter as the tension increased. We were still some distance from our destination.

With agonizing slowness we kept moving until finally the airport was in sight. When we finally reached the terminal, Mother, the children, and I rushed to the check-in desk, breathless, only to hear that the flight had just left. I was in shock.

Clutching my baby, I said frantically, "My husband is going to the Pacific and I must say good-bye to him!"

A look of desperation must have been on my face. The agent looked at me thoughtfully for what seemed an eternity and then said abruptly, "How much do you weigh, lady?"

Surprised, I answered "One hundred and twelve pounds."

"Come with me," said the agent.

By now my Dad had arrived with our suitcase after parking the car. We all followed the agent to a scale nearby. The children and I were weighed along with my small suitcase. There was a consultation among three or four other men with the man from the counter. Finally, he turned to me with a big smile and said, "OK, lady, we'll get you there to see your husband."

After a hug and good-bye to my parents, we were put on an airplane that had regular seats but no other passengers. I looked around, puzzled. Suddenly I realized why we had been weighed. We were on a plane taking cargo to Chicago. I guess as long as we didn't weigh too much they could take us along with the cargo!

I had never flown before, and this is one memory I will never forget. I took a deep breath, settled Bruce into his seat and held baby Richard tightly as we lifted into the air—the cargo, the children, and I.

My memory of the Chicago Airport is dim, but I was not bumped off my flight to Mobile as I changed airplanes from my "cargo express." As for the cargo, I never knew what they were carrying—except us!

The children and I stepped off the plane in Mobile into a mild, sunny day with the scent of flowers in the air. I never dreamed there could be such a place in December! At that moment I fell in love with the South and Mobile in particular.

And most of all, there was my husband. I had shut the door of my house in Mankato expecting to be back in a matter of weeks. I never saw it again.

4

Mobile, Alabama, and Greenville, Mississippi

We settled into temporary quarters at Brookley Air Base, waiting for the orders which were due in a short time. Within a few weeks they came. But to our surprise the orders to the Pacific were canceled. Shippy was to remain in Mobile for the time being. What joy this brought to my heart!

At once we started to look for housing. There was no room at the base, and we were extremely fortunate to find a nice rental home on Mobile Bay. I don't remember how we managed to get clothes and other such things, but the house was furnished and we were happy and blessed to be together. In those wartime days, we lived one day at a time.

As for our house in Mankato, the owner eventually sold it. My parents had to drive from Minneapolis and put all our things in storage. How much I owed my dear mother and dad. I often wonder what happened to all the fruits and vegetables I had preserved so painstakingly that were lined up on shelves in the basement. I never thought to ask my mother.

Back in Mobile, I discovered some new challenges of living in the South. I had, of course, been reading my Bible. 1 Thessalonians 5:18 impressed me, and I was doing my best "to give thanks for everything for this is the will of God concerning you." I thought I was doing well until I made the acquaintance of several different creatures that I had never encountered in Minnesota. There were the large flying roaches that I found awesome and intimidating, as their demise demanded a frontal and courageous attack. Then there were small ants that would appear insidiously in various, odd places, including—to my astonished eyes—my children's clothing.

Responding to this crisis, my husband arrived one day from the base looking like an escapee from outer space with a huge tank on his back. That was the end of the ants. Reveling in this victory, I went to the kitchen one morning to see, with horrified eyes, the entire sink covered with winged creatures. The termites were swarming, I was told!

And then there were the mice. Here I must confess I met my Waterloo. For some strange reason embedded in my primitive past, there lurks an intense dislike of mice over which I have no control. I dealt with them by setting the traps and then giving Bruce five cents for each trap he emptied. (Don't ask me where.) Actually, it worked out very well.

Believe it or not, I found out in years to come that my giving thanks for all the creepy crawlers and fliers was truly well founded. The good Lord was doing me a favor by making me confront these creatures at an early age. In later years, my family and I were to live in Egypt. To my delight, I was perfectly at home with all the little creatures there. I could flip the weevils out of the flour with nary a thought and felt quite friendly with the roaches (though they were not as large as the Mobile variety and did not fly!).

Adjusting to life in Mobile was a pleasure. Our time in Mobile Bay was happy, war or no war. The flowers were a delight. I was enchanted by the camellias; I had never seen a lovelier flower. The sweet smelling jasmine was at our back door, and the Bay was at our front door, accessible for catching crabs that we put into the delicious gumbo our neighbors taught us to make.

But most blessed of all to us were our next-door neighbors, Mrs. S, a recent widow, and her daughter Betsy. Betsy loved our children and spent time with them, especially the baby. They were a second mother and sister to me, and I will never forget them. I returned with Bruce to see them a few years after the war had ended.

At a later time our entire family drove to Mobile for a visit. The beauty of the "Azalea Trail," the camellias, and Government Street—the main road through Mobile—will remain a treasure in my heart forever.

A last mention of my eye problem. It was still troubling me, and I finally went to a doctor to have it checked. The only possible causes the doctor could find were my tonsils and a rectal infection. So into the hospital I went to have my tonsils removed and the rectal infection treated. I had ice on one end and heat on the other!

There was no immediate change in my eye, but gradually the infection improved. I mention this because it was an important step in my Quest. My eye was my "thorn in the flesh." Paul's words from the Lord were carved into my soul, "My grace is sufficient for you. My strength is made perfect in weakness," (2 Cor. 12:9 KJV).

The Lord was now also my *teacher* as well as Paul's. I had to live by His grace until He felt I was safely dependent on Him and would not stray too far from His side, for there would be difficult days ahead.

After about a year and a half in Mobile, we received orders transferring us to Greenville, Mississippi. It was difficult to leave our house on Mobile Bay and especially hard to say good-bye to Mrs. S and Betsy.

Our stay in Greenville was short, but I have happy memories of our Thanksgiving dinner at the base. I also enjoyed the mild southern weather in November, so different from my days in Minnesota at that time of year. We found an apartment, with some difficulty, but it was adequate and we adjusted to our new environment.

In January, my husband arranged a surprise birthday party at the base. There was an enormous cake that I will never forget. We shared it with everyone in the dining room!

The war was now in its final stages, and we were eventually transferred back to Mobile. One memory is vivid from that time, and that was our deep concern when we heard the news of the Battle of the Bulge. We flocked to crowded churches to pray. Fortunately, this ferocious battle was the last gasp for the Germans. The war was ending.

5

A Dark Period

We left Greenville and returned to Mobile but had great difficulty finding a place to stay. The war was winding down but housing was still scarce. We stayed for a short time with Mrs. S and Betsy while we kept looking, but nothing could I find. I made the decision to go home to Minneapolis. My husband had no objection, as he was hoping to be released from active duty before too long.

It was the worst decision I have ever made, and I suffered deeply from it—physically and emotionally. The clue to it all was that *I* had made the decision. I had not prayed to ask Jesus to direct me, nor had my husband and I prayed together requesting His guidance in our decision. How I thought I could go "home" to Minneapolis when I had no home to go to is beyond my understanding. I learned a lesson I will never forget.

We moved in initially with my parents, but they did not have room in their duplex to keep the boys and me indefinitely. Fortunately, after about a month, the manse of my church became available for a limited time. Our furniture was taken out of storage and we moved in.

My health, my energy, and my spirits were at a low ebb. I went to the Lord on my hands and knees in great need and prayed for help. In answer, I was led to Proverbs 3:6: "In all your ways acknowledge Him and He will direct your paths." During those months in Minneapolis before my husband was released from service, those words were branded on my soul. I knew Jesus' *name,* and I knew Him as a *friend* and *helper.* But I did not yet know Him as a *master*. From that time forward I never made a decision of any importance in my life without laying it out before Him and asking Him to guide me to the right decision. I realized that He, and He alone, had wisdom that I did not have. He was teaching me to give over the reins of my life to Him. I also understood that giving my will over to Him would be continually tested. I needed discipline to stay close to Him, to let Him really become my *master,* as well as to know him by *name* and as a *friend* and *helper*. This is where my Quest now led me.

"My grace is sufficient for you for My strength is made perfect in weakness" (2 Cor. 12:9 KJV). These words were carved on my heart. "In all your ways acknowledge Him and He shall direct your paths," (Prov. 3:6 KJV). That verse was branded there with the hot iron of deep need.

6

The GI Bill

Finally the war was over, and the waiting came to an end. Shippy was released from active duty, and with his return, my spirits lifted. The major responsibility for life in general and the children in particular was once again shared.

Unfortunately, the housing problem had still not been solved. Our time in the manse was coming to an end, and we had to move. We looked with single-minded concentration but could find nothing. At last we came across a small house in southeast Minneapolis that only desperation would cause us to consider. It had been built entirely by hand of some sort of material (your guess is as good as mine), and there were few walls that came together squarely or evenly. The floors were covered with linoleum under which I never dared to look. It came at last to a decision to buy that "odd house" (which we named it) or go into a Quonset hut. As strange as the house was, it was still better than a Quonset hut (as anyone who has seen a Quonset hut can attest). So we bought it. The best thing we could say for it was that it was affordable! The last thing we discovered when we moved in was that the house was built on a bog and was settling slowly but inevitably into the ground.

Shippy and I started to work on the house shortly after we moved in. He put up wallpaper, which was indeed a challenge. No walls came together evenly, and the paper was more often around his neck than on the wall. He persevered, and in the end the result was presentable. Our furniture and rugs were still in good condition, in spite of storage, and we settled in, thankful that we were in a house, albeit a very odd one.

The house also had a strange bathroom that toddler Richard did not like at all. It was small and had a folding door. I would fold it back for him and in he would go with very tentative cooperation. Closing the folding door was more traumatic, but in time he came (from necessity) to terms with it. Apparently he had no major traumas from the door as he eventually became a Navy pilot landing on aircraft carriers. I guess his nerves withstood the folding-door trauma.

My husband had decided to take advantage of the GI Bill, a tuition-assistance program offered by the government to help returning veterans continue their education. Shippy enrolled at the University of Minnesota to study for his Master's Degree. I, too, enrolled in an evening class at the university, as my husband would be home at nights to look after the boys. I am interested in history, so I signed up for a class in Twentieth Century Europe. It was my extremely good fortune that the teacher of that evening class was one of the best history professors at the university. He had been with the Office of Strategic Services (OSS), later known as the CIA, during the war, and he inspired me to start work on a master's degree in history.

He often commented what a joy it was for him to teach that particular evening class filled with mature, war-weary veterans (plus me!) hungry to learn and get on with their lives. It was a privilege to be part of that class.

The year ended, my husband received his degree, and we survived without the house sinking into the bog. We sold the house as quickly as possible and were very fortunate to find a lovely home on a tree-lined boulevard in northeast Minneapolis. My husband was most relieved to be out of our "odd house" before disaster struck in one form or another.

On moving day the driver stopped the truck at our new address and looked at me in a puzzled way.

"Are you sure this is the right place, lady?"

"Oh, very sure indeed," I replied. "Isn't it lovely?" I felt like Lois in Wonderland, magically lifted out of that very odd house!

7

The Korean War

We settled into our new house, and Shippy went to work as a regional engineer with the Minnesota Department of Health. We had about four serene and happy years. Then, unexpectedly, came the next crisis.

On July 25, 1950, the forces of the People's Republic of Korea (North Korea) invaded the Republic of Korea (South Korea). The United States introduced a resolution in the Security Council of the United Nations urging U.N. members to contribute such assistance as might be needed to repel the aggressors.

Responding to the U.N. appeal, twenty governments eventually sent combat forces or medical contingents, which were called United Nations Civil Assistance Commands. The United States was asked for help, especially for these medical units. Shippy's chief was contacted and asked if he could suggest any public health engineers who might be interested in serving in Korea for one year as part of a medical team. He approached Shippy.

My husband would not have volunteered to serve in World War II without my consent, so of course he sought out my agreement on this idea as well. But, unlike in World War II, this time I reacted forcefully against his going. I felt as if I would like to get on the floor and kick and scream and beat my feet and fists against anything within my reach.

Only one thing kept me in control, and that was the lesson I had learned at the end of the war. "In all your ways acknowledge Him and He will direct your paths," (Prov. 3:6). That verse of scripture had been branded on my soul, so I went to prayer.

With great inner struggle, I came to the place where I told Jesus I would accept whatever direction He would lead me in—let Shippy go to Korea or stay for my sake and the boys' well being.

The answer came. I knew in my inner depths that I had to let him go. I had to say yes for this one year. Don't ask me how I knew, but I did know that I was obeying my Master. I did not know *why* I had to say yes, but it became very clear that I must do so.

He left and the year passed. My parents and family roots were in Minneapolis, so I was not bereft of love and support. I was especially blessed with three neighbors on our block who became life-long friends. They gave me Christian love, fellowship, and support. I learned patience and endurance. We shared Shippy's life in Korea by mail as his letters came regularly. I have kept all my letters from my husband during his year in Korea and have given some of them to Bruce to read. I will eventually give them all to the boys to touch their father and read his words during that year he was away from us.

We were united a year later. Once more I gave thanks to God.

Approximately a year after Shippy's homecoming, I realized why I had to agree to the year in Korea. Based largely on contacts he had made in Korea, my husband was recruited by the World Health Organization of the United Nations for an assignment in Ankara, Turkey. That year in Korea opened up a vista of world-wide scope for Shippy's work and career and created a new life for our family. As for me, I was about to begin the happiest years of my life as the whole world opened before me. The Lord gave me a "rainbow in the sky" when he revealed to me why I had to say yes. My horizons of mind and spirit were to be broadened and expanded, and I thrilled to the excitement and the challenge of the world before me. I had obeyed (albeit reluctantly) when Jesus led me down a difficult path. I was now ready and willing as we prepared to leave for Turkey in September 1952.

Part Two:
The Innocents Abroad

8

Turkey and "Listening"

Once again I was leaving my house, locking the door behind me, flying into the unknown, and—déjà vu—I was nevermore to live there. But I *did* see it again!

There was one important difference this time. We owned the property, so I would not experience the insecurity of having no home where I could return. I refused to allow my husband to sell that house in Minneapolis until six years later, when we returned from overseas and purchased another house in our new location, Chevy Chase, Maryland. Only then would I relinquish my security blanket!

Aside from the movers dropping the piano as part of our furniture was being sent into storage, our exit was accomplished without undue stress. It was difficult to say good-bye to my parents and the neighbors with whom I had become close friends. As our Boeing Stratocruiser lifted into the air from Wold Chamberlin Field, I waved a last farewell to Minneapolis. We were on our way to New York to board the ocean liner *Queen Elizabeth*, bound for the port of Cherbourg, France, and then on to Paris by train. Richard, eight years old, and Bruce, about to turn eleven, were delighted with the airplane. They had never flown before (except for their experience on the "cargo express"), and it was indeed an impressive beginning. They explored the stairs leading to the lower lounge in the Stratocruiser with great enthusiasm. As for me, I loved to fly, which was a good thing with the number of miles I would log in the future!

Crossing the Atlantic for the first time on the *Queen Elizabeth* was an experience in a dream world. I have to admit that for me there can never be too many crystal chandeliers, red carpets, or elegant dinners. I blend into it all with the greatest of ease! Oh, yes, I remember Ecclesiastes 2:1: "Vanity, vanity, all is vanity." But for five days, I enjoyed every minute of this luxury.

Richard's favorite spot was the large room with a painting of Queen Elizabeth, the Queen Mother. However, what drew him there at teatime were the delicious chocolate éclairs. Bruce's energies were directed to exploring all areas of the ship, undaunted by whether or not access was allowed. I donned a different gown every evening for dinner, and although I was not as lovely as "the lilies of the field" in the Bible, I felt quite presentable. What an unforgettable experience as we were truly the "innocents" on our way abroad!

All dreams must come to an end. We arrived in Cherbourg, France, left the ship by tender and boarded a train for Paris. There we enjoyed a guided tour, with a rather reluctant Richard, as I remember, but I marveled at the wonder and beauty that is Paris.

Leaving the "City of Light," we flew to Rome for a memorable few days before departing for Geneva, Switzerland, where Shippy was to be briefed on his work in Turkey. Geneva was a delightful city with flowers everywhere, including the lampposts. The city embraced beautiful Lake Geneva, home to graceful swans, fed by Bruce and Richard with bread saved from dinner. Just writing the word *dinner* brings to mind the delicious food in Switzerland. The aroma of the bread alone cast a spell, to say nothing of its taste.

The croissants were made in heaven, and we spent many hours in their celestial company!

While Shippy was being briefed at World Health Organization (WHO) headquarters, friends took the boys and me up a cable car to nearby Mont Saleve. There we enjoyed a picnic lunch, flew kites, played "king of the mountain," enjoyed the spectacular view, and had a wonderful time. Trite words, you might say, and rightfully so. But remember, we were the "innocents abroad," so we had our privileges and could be exuberant!

The day came to depart, and "the innocents" were to begin their first assignment abroad. We flew out of the Geneva Airport, the first of many times we would be flying into and out of that impressive airport. Our destination: Ankara, Turkey.

The capital of Turkey had been moved from Istanbul to Ankara, so there was a great deal of construction in the city when we arrived. We were able to find an apartment in a new building and immediately started to look for the necessities of living, as we had brought no furniture with us. In a short time, we were able to transform the apartment into livable quarters, with attractive local materials for draperies and adequate furniture. And, just as our physical circumstances were improving, so was our spiritual life.

We became friends with the chaplain of the American forces stationed in Ankara. As part of his church program he started a small group for Bible study, Christian fellowship, and support. This was my first experience living abroad in a different culture, and I welcomed the opportunity to belong to this group. It was there that I first heard of "listening."

The chaplain challenged us to spend time in quiet each morning reading the Word of God, praying, and interceding. But he also urged us to set aside some minutes just to be still and *listen*. He emphasized that our focus was to be on Jesus, our one true way to salvation, and we were to turn our thoughts to Him alone. As Psalm 16:8 says so beautifully, "I have set the Lord always before me; because He is at my right hand, I shall not be moved."

We were instructed to take pencil and paper and experiment with writing down thoughts as they came to our mind. The chaplain explained that God speaks to us in our thoughts but that we easily forget what He says, so it helps to write it down. Scripture tells us time after time how God spoke to His people, guiding and directing them. We were to learn to live in close companionship with Jesus, our Savior, and learn to *know* Him, not just *about* Him. I started to listen, haltingly and intermittently at first. In later years this became a discipline lovingly anticipated each morning until, like author Brother Lawrence, "I accustomed myself to a familiar, humble, affectionate conversation with Jesus."

Brother Lawrence—born Nicholas Herman in French Lorranine—became a lay Brother among the Carmelites of Paris. His letters and conversations, first published in French in 1692, have become a Christian classic, titled "The Practice of the Presence of God."

The chaplain also gave us these excerpts from men of God on listening and conversing with Jesus.

From Brother Lawrence's book *The Practice of the Presence of God*: "You would think it rude to leave a friend alone who came to visit you; why then must Jesus be neglected?" And, "We must accustom ourselves to a familiar, humble, affectionate conversation with Him."

From Oswald Chambers' book *My Utmost for His Highest*: "The measure of the worth of our public activity for God is the private, profound communication we have with him."

I am grateful for that small group in Turkey and the army chaplain who opened for us a pathway into deeper and more intimate fellowship with our Lord. However irregular and intermittent my listening was at first, in time it became a cherished conversation with a friend and Master who promised me He would never "leave me or forsake me," (KJV). My spiritual Quest was leading me into those "green pastures and still waters" that I knew not as I repeated the Twenty-third Psalm so fearfully the day of Bruce's birth.

In later years, I wrote a letter to a young mother on listening. I am including it here, hoping that it may be helpful to others who may be seeking a closer walk with Jesus.

> Dearest Jean,
>
> The times of our greatest needs are always the times of our greatest growth in the Lord. Of all His gifts to us, the one of closeness to Him is the most precious. We must each one find for ourselves that personal relationship which bonds us as a child to its father, the great Heavenly Father who is the only one who can meet our deepest needs.
>
> This is a personal journey that only we ourselves can initiate. We must discipline ourselves to seek and find communion with Him. My own journey started years ago, and it demanded perseverance to *listen* for that voice of Jesus. He will speak to us in our thoughts when we are quiet before Him.
>
> Find a copy of the great Christian classic *The Practice of the Presence* by Brother Lawrence, and soak in it! Take small quiet moments when you can arrange them, and just tell Jesus your needs and your problems. Praise and thank Him, even if you feel you have nothing for which to give thanks. Make it a true "sacrifice" of thanksgiving. Thank Him that He uses painful situations and suffering to bring good to us. His ways are not our ways. His plans for us are for good and not for evil. We must trust Him and praise Him.

> Take a small notebook, and when possible, even for short periods, find a quiet place to be alone. Talk to Him like the friend and Father He is. Give Him your burdens one by one. Then be quiet and ask Him to speak to you and guide and direct you. Write down any thoughts that come to your mind. They may seem useless, and if only one thought comes, write it down.
>
> Persevere. Do not be discouraged as, day by day, you write down little or nothing. He *will* speak and you will find your little notebook growing with His words of wisdom and love.
>
> Dearest Jean, I can give you no more precious guidance than Eli gave to Samuel in the Scriptures, 1 Samuel 3:9–10: "Go, lie down and it shall be, if He calls you, that you must say, 'Speak Lord, for your servant hears.' So Samuel went and lay down in his place.
>
> "Now the Lord came and called as at other times, Samuel, Samuel.' And Samuel answered, 'Speak, Lord, for your servant hears.'"
>
> Jean, dearest, when He calls, "Jean, Jean," He wants to hear, "Speak Lord, for your servant hears."

When I think back on Turkey, the concept of listening was certainly the strongest spiritual memory I have. But almost as strong a memory was the excitement of our first foreign travel and discovering new lands and cultures beyond our own.

I regret that I was not able to revisit Turkey in later years and see the wonders of modern growth and reconstruction which have taken place there. Its oriental splendor shone forth before my eyes so long ago in the magnificent palaces of Topkapi and Dohlmabace, along with the Blue Mosque and Hagia Sophia. The bazaars were intriguing, thronged with people in native and modern dress, creating an ever-changing montage of vivid colors worthy of an artist's palette. Turkey is one of Bruce's favorite countries, and he has returned many times, revisiting and enjoying its treasures.

After fourteen months in Turkey, Shippy was transferred to Cairo, Egypt. We would return to Minnesota for a brief home leave in December 1953 and then set out for our new assignment. In that ancient land of Egypt awaited many new experiences—and one unexpected crisis. Meanwhile, my spiritual Quest continued. Jesus was now someone I knew personally, but I still needed to grow and mature. There would be challenges to meet, for which I was unprepared.

9

SS Excambion and Egypt

Before leaving Turkey permanently, we flew to Cairo, where World Health Organization staff members showed us the area where we might live and also briefed my husband on the village project where he would work. In conjunction with this trip, we visited the island of Cypress, Beirut (Lebanon), and Jerusalem before returning to Turkey. I was enchanted with the Crusader Castle of St. Hilarion on Cypress, which we visited one sunny day during that summer of 1953. We climbed the stony path to the ruins, rising over two thousand feet above the sea. There I had my picture taken in the "Queen's Window" at the peak. According to legend, Richard the Lionheart went forth from this castle to the Crusades.

We stayed in a hotel in Nicosia, the capital of Cypress, which had a delightful and large terrace. There we had our evening meals, including a special dinner celebrating our fifteenth wedding anniversary (on August 22) and Richard's ninth birthday, which came later in the month. The boys gave us a surprise gift of native, embroidered place mats. They are treasured to this day.

Beirut, Lebanon, was especially lovely in the early '50s. We enjoyed the Mediterranean Sea and were intrigued with the large, blue jellyfish! The ancient ruins of Baalbek were an imposing reminder of the power of Rome, and the

"Cedars of Lebanon" brought back memories of King Solomon's temple, adorned with wood from the famous, great trees of Lebanon. I am sad when I read of the fighting there that has caused such devastation and suffering.

Our travel in Jerusalem was limited by restrictions on our passports. Since we carried Arab visas, we could not travel as freely as we wished. However, we toured Bethlehem, said prayers at the Wailing Wall in Jerusalem, and visited sacred sites such as the Garden of Gethsemane, the Dome of the Rock, and the Garden Tomb. I had thought that I would surely return, but Shippy's work was eventually transferred to other parts of the world, and it did not work out for me to revisit the Holy Land.

In the late fall of 1953, we said our permanent goodbye to Turkey and flew to Geneva, Switzerland. We then boarded a train to Paris, where we were scheduled for a flight to New York for our first home leave. Unfortunately, there was a strike at the Paris Airport, so we were rerouted to Brussels, Belgium. At last we soared into the air for our homeward journey to spend Christmas with our family in Minneapolis.

Home leave was a happy time of reunion with family, friends, and neighbors. One day flowed into another, filled with shared experiences, visits, and shopping. The time passed all too quickly, and soon it was time to return overseas. Again, it was not easy to leave my parents or my brother and his family of six children.

In February 1954, I left alone by train to New York. Shippy and the boys drove our new Chevrolet Bel Air (which we were shipping to Egypt) to New York, where we were scheduled to rendezvous. The train trip and separate travel arrangements were necessary due to our volume of baggage!

Once reunited in New York, we boarded the liner *Excambion* for our second voyage across the ocean. The *Excambion* was smaller and less formal than the *Queen Elizabeth*, but we enjoyed its intimate atmosphere. Again, we waved good-bye to the Statue of Liberty as we slowly sailed away to our new destination, Egypt. We encountered some rough weather at the start of our journey, but it did not dim our enthusiasm! One evening at dinner we thought we were managing the rough weather quite well until our chairs started to slide, with us in them, from one side of the dining room to the other, and then back to our table with us still intact!

I have one especially vivid memory from the crossing. I decided to go out on deck late one afternoon. There was only one other man at the railing. We stood there mesmerized by the power, beauty, and ferocity of the waves. They rose to great heights and then fell into a cascade of colors—jade, indigo, and white intermingled. The waves were an awesome sight as they rose and fell in hypnotic rhythm. I can't recall how long we stood there, holding the railing, soaring up and down with each wave. It was a "time out of time." I finally left, reluctantly, to take my place at the dinner table. I was one of the few who made it to the dining room! And, I might add, despite being the only member of the "weaker sex" in our family, I was the one who was never seasick on our four crossings.

The waters became calm once we reached the Mediterranean, and the rest of the trip was delightful. The boys initiated a petition to fill the swimming pool, which had remained empty across the Atlantic due to the cold February waters. The petition succeeded, but only a few shivering bodies went for a swim, including, of course, Bruce and Richard, the instigators.

We went ashore at Barcelona, Spain; Marseilles, France; and Naples, Italy. The Naples visit included an awe-inspiring tour of Pompeii, the town buried alive by the volcanic eruption of Mount Vesuvius centuries before.

All in all, it was a happy and relaxed crossing, and after three weeks the *Excambion* had truly become a home to us. However, the Alexandria Harbor was coming into view, signaling the end of our journey. Although the Great Lighthouse of Alexandria, which was one of the seven wonders of the ancient world, was no longer there, our entrance to the harbor was still impressive. We disembarked with mixed feelings, reluctant to be leaving our sheltered existence and happy time on the ship but eager to set foot on Egyptian soil and start our new assignment. We were about to begin our unforgettable years in Egypt.

10

Egypt and Home Leave

We drove to Cairo in the car we had brought with us and stayed the night at the old Semiramis Hotel, a picturesque landmark which has since been demolished and rebuilt.

We started looking for suitable housing in Maadi, a small town near Cairo where we hoped to live. In time, we discovered a new apartment building with the top floor apartment available. We rented it at once. Our furniture came in due time, and we settled comfortably into this charming little town.

There was a club with a swimming pool, tennis courts, and movie theater. The boys went to an American school, which was housed in a former palace. I melded into the atmosphere and delighted in the Jacaranda trees with their delicate clusters of lavender blossoms. The stage was set for my entry into a new world.

Egypt's history and archeological wonders were rich treasures that we explored with family trips to the pyramids of Giza, the tombs of Luxor, Mount Sinai, and the Red Sea. However, we had not come to Egypt on a holiday excursion. My husband was part of a World Health Organization team of doctors, nurses, and experienced public health workers who joined with Egyptian experts working to improve the health and life of the villagers. Shippy's expertise was in water-borne diseases. In the Egyptian projects he worked on a program to control schistosomiasis, a chronic and usually tropical disease caused by parasites.

My first introduction to the head of Shippy's WHO team, with whom he would be working in the villages, was at a meeting he had planned for team members and families shortly after our arrival. The team leader, Dr. K., was from Zagreb, which was then in Yugoslavia. He spoke of the need in the villages for improved health care facilities, better sanitation, nourishing food, and medical attention. I agreed with him wholeheartedly. He then, to my consternation, concluded with a denunciation of Christian missionaries. He asserted that what the villagers needed was what he had emphasized, not some "pie in the sky" beliefs the missionaries could give them.

I am not a person who likes confrontation. I was still, if not a "baby Christian," at best a young one. I look back at this episode to this day with amazement. I found myself rising to my feet when he had finished. Exactly what I said or how much I said I do not remember. I only recall that I quoted Deuteronomy 8:3, "Man shall not live by bread alone, but man lives by every word that proceeds from the mouth of the Lord." I spoke my piece, and no one was more surprised than myself, except perhaps my husband. However, Shippy was a secure man and, although astonished, he was not troubled by my remarks. The real surprise was Dr. K.'s reaction. After the meeting he came to a place where Shippy and I were talking to others. He shook my hand, looked into my eyes, and said, "That was interesting what you said about the missionaries. Sometime I would like to talk to you about the Bible."

Thus began a treasured friendship between Dr. K., his wife and daughter, and our family. He and I did have talks together from time to time about the Bible. His questions were not easy to answer in my embryonic stage of Christian faith and knowledge. I remember he challenged me about the Bible not speaking out against slavery.

I became a close friend to Dr. K.'s lovely blond, blue-eyed, teenage daughter, Miki. I remember she asked me to bring her a ruffled petticoat from the United States when we returned from our next home leave. The '50s were the era of big skirts, and fancy petticoats were in fashion. I returned with the most be-ruffled petticoat I could find, and she was ecstatic!

In future years, when we were living in Chevy Chase, Maryland, Dr. K. stayed with us many times when he came to Washington as a consultant with the World Bank. We later had an opportunity to visit Dr. K.'s family in Zagreb in conjunction with a World Bank assignment given to Shippy. (I was allowed to accompany him on certain trips, based on the number of days he was away from home—one of many perks that made Shippy's future employer, the World Bank, a great place to work.) During this visit, daughter Miki was in the midst of an emotional crisis, and the entire family was suffering. I had taken with me Hannah Whithall Smith's book *A Christian's Secret of a Happy Life*. Miki and I had long talks together, and when I left, I gave her my copy. She recovered and is now happily married. In later years, she visited us in Chevy Chase for six months, with her husband joining her for the last few months.

Dr. K told me he had fought under Tito in World War II. He smiled and added, "My nickname was Cobra." Dr. K. has died, but Miki and her mother are still at the same home in Zagreb. Bruce has visited them and spent time with the family. The K. family enriched our lives, and we are thankful for their friendship.

Other friendships we developed in Egypt—very different from the K. family's, but just as real—were with our

Egyptian servants. This new life I had entered included servants. I accepted them, endeavored to adjust to them (and they to me) and learned from them. Finally I grew to cherish them, especially Shafik, our second servant.

The first servant we had on arriving in Maadi was Mohammed. My most vivid memory of Mohammed stemmed from a visit to his house. He invited me to visit his home in the village to celebrate the birth of a new child. He had whitewashed the walls of his home and carefully prepared tea for me. With pride he showed me his new baby. He and his wife were happy to have me as their guest, and it was a visit I will never forget. How much we take for granted the privileges we enjoy in America. I was humbled by the hospitality of Mohammed and his wife and the preparation they had made for my visit.

A few weeks later, Mohammed came up to me as I was leaving for an appointment. Quietly he said, "The baby has died. Praise be to Allah. It is written."

Mohammed was drafted into the Egyptian Army and left soon after. His replacement, Shafik, remained our servant for the duration of our stay. Shafik was a Coptic Christian and spoke fair English. He was a good man, and I respected him. He was also a good cook. Every Sunday we had lamb and homemade ice cream, which Shafik would produce after much labor of stirring the mixture by hand. Shafik respected me and tolerated me, but it was my husband to whom he gave his first allegiance. "*Malish*," as they say in Arabic. "So be it, accept it gracefully." And I did.

We had frequent guests in Egypt, and Shafik looked forward to entertaining them almost as much as we did. He would put on his best galabia (traditional long robe) and serve in his best style, which was indeed elegant. The more company we had, the better he liked it. He could then get extra help and be the majordomo. In later years, we moved into a house with a large garden, many flowers, a small pool with fish, statues, and large poinsettias. He ruled with great pleasure over two gardeners, an ironing man, a wash lady, and extras when we had guests. Shaifik was a good man, and he became a longtime friend.

I mentioned before that the stage was set for my entry into a new world. Indeed, it was a new world and the description "stage" is very apt. From my first step on Egyptian soil upon arriving in Alexandria until I left, I never ceased to marvel at this new life I was living. The flowering trees of Maadi were the backdrops, and all Egypt—from the desert to the Nile, from the ancient tombs of the Valley of the Kings at Luxor to the pyramids—was on a grand scale, and they were all parts of my new world. I felt at times I was living my life in a movie or in the world of the theater. I also knew and experienced a less romantic reaction upon seeing a different life experienced by others, especially when I visited the village where my husband worked. But the lure of the Middle East had touched my soul.

I have many memories from my years in Egypt, some happy, some sad, but all vivid. Here, in no particular order, are some of the memories that stand out.

Richard began playing tennis at the club to which we belonged in Maadi. One of his teachers was a former member of the Egyptian Davis Cup team. Because of this excellent instruction, the opportunity to play year-round and his enthusiasm for the game, he became a good player and started to play in some tournaments. Every year, the American Embassy in Cairo sponsored a tennis tournament for all Americans living there. Both Richard and my husband entered. To my dismay, they became the finalists!

The day came and the match was close. (Richard was eleven years old.) I sat there in a state, like my mother, and

I vowed I would never speak to my husband again if he beat Richard, but I knew all the time he was so competitive he would never consider not playing his best. It was a terrible time for me. I finally could stand it no longer and left, but I knew I had to return before the match ended, as they wanted to take my picture with the winner. I returned for the final deciding set, shutting my eyes most of the time. Upon opening them, I saw the American ambassador's wife presenting the cup to Richard and beckoning me to come for a picture with him.

I arose and walked toward them with a happy smile on my face, but little did they know what I had been through, nor did my husband realize what dangerous waters of rejection he had been in!

While in Egypt I made use of my degree from the College of Education at the University of Minnesota in several different ways. I taught classes at the Cairo-American school in Junior High English and Social Studies. I also worked as the school librarian. In addition, I taught Sunday School at the little church in Maadi that we attended. With a friend, we made puppets for a summer children's project that was received with great enthusiasm by the children.

One of my most rewarding tasks was teaching the Bible to a class for girls in the Egyptian school nearby. They were Christians and were released for an hour of Bible study while the Muslim children studied the Koran. A missionary friend of mine was the regular teacher, but she became ill and had to leave Egypt. She asked me if I would teach the class in her place. There were about eight-to-ten girls, ages eight to twelve, and they were a class that was a teacher's dream. I would look into their eyes, and they would be drinking in everything I had been saying. All the spiritual hunger of the people in an area of the world that has produced three great religions was reflected in their eyes. I kept in touch with them after I returned to the States, but eventually we lost contact. I wish I could have been with them longer. They share a place among my most precious memories of Egypt.

In a lighter vein was a family trip we took with friends to Hurghada, a Red Sea resort area known for its beautiful coral and colorful underwater life. We did only snorkeling, but it was a beautiful and exciting experience. As I put on my headgear and went underwater, small zebra fish in unbelievable numbers were darting in and out around my feet. Everything was pulsating with life and energy, creating a kaleidoscope of changing images before my astonished eyes. The sunlight reflecting on the water melded the colors into a potpourri of brilliant hues and delicate pastels. No sunken treasure of gold or silver could compare with this world around me. The angelfish and strange sea creatures glowed with iridescent brilliance as they flashed through the water. I gazed with wonder at this world of unearthly beauty before me. I lost all track of time. How long I stayed in the water I do not remember. I do remember, however, seeing a huge white fish swimming in my direction. It was then I left with alacrity!

Shafik, our servant, was delighted to come with us. It was an opportunity for him to expand his horizons, and I remember how he enjoyed wading in the Red Sea, his long galabia pulled high to keep dry. He cooked our meals, which were simple, and we helped. I understand that today large luxury hotels have replaced the simple lodging we enjoyed in the '50s, but surely the underwater life is as beautiful as ever.

Another experience we all enjoyed were picnics at the Great Pyramids of Giza. Many friends visited us while we were in Egypt, and often we took them to supper at the Pyramids. They always were delighted, even though they had to sit on and eat off of big rocks. I had taught Shafik three Betty Crocker recipes of basic meals, and we would alternate them from one visitor to another. They were gala times, and we loved entertaining and sharing our life in Egypt with them.

In January 1955, we boarded the train to Luxor for a much-anticipated visit to the Valley of the Kings, where the ancient Pharaohs were buried. We were also looking forward to seeing the famous Temple of Karnak.

Our hotel in Luxor was a comfortable building resting on the banks of the Nile River. Surrounded by a fragrant garden, it welcomed us graciously, and we settled in for a long weekend. I also sank into a huge bed every night, enveloped in mosquito netting for the first time (remember, this was the '50s before air conditioning was common in Egypt). The majestic pillars of Karnak greeted us the next day as we arose early and started our sightseeing. We had an excellent guide who was determined we would not miss anything that was important, at least in his eyes! A long row of sphinx lined the avenue to the Temple. The overpowering size of the ancient columns and the inscriptions on them that had endured through endless time gave one an awesome admiration for the gifts and skill of these remarkable people who created them. We crossed the Nile to the Valley of the Kings, accompanied by the rhythmic chanting of the oarsmen. A car met us, and we were told (true or untrue, I do not know) that archeologist Howard Carter had used it when he was excavating King Tutankhamen's tomb. We visited all the tombs we had time and strength to see. It was a weekend never to be forgotten, and I especially cherished the opportunity to share it together as a family. I said very quietly to myself under my breath, "Thank you, World Health Organization, for sending us to Egypt!"

The days and months slipped by, and soon it was time for our second home leave, June 1956. We flew to Geneva, Switzerland, where we took the train through the Simplon Tunnel and along the beautiful Italian Riviera to Milan, Italy. From there we traveled to Genoa where we boarded the SS *Independence* for our crossing to New York. We had a smooth and pleasant voyage with many activities on board, particularly for the boys. We sailed into New York and disembarked into that great city that always causes my adrenaline to surge.

Just a few weeks later, the new Italian ship *Andrea Doria*, also sailing from Genoa to New York, sank following a collision at sea. On board that ship were friends of ours from Egypt who had been with us at the Red Sea and later filled us in on the details of the accident. Fortunately, they were unhurt and most of the other passengers were rescued. We had considered taking this ship, but as it sailed a few weeks later than we wished to depart, we decided on the *Independence* instead.

As usual on home leave, the days took wings filled with family and friends to see and shopping to accomplish. My father had died, but my mother was well as were my brother and his family. All too soon, it was time to return to Egypt. It was a bittersweet reunion without my father, but life goes on.

In August 1956, we left Minneapolis for New York where we boarded KLM Royal Dutch Airlines headed for Amsterdam, Holland. In Amsterdam, we visited vast fields of tulips that seemed to encompass us, and we took a trip on a canal barge that was fun and relaxing.

Not so relaxing was the news that Gamal Abdul Nasser, the President of Egypt, had seized the Suez Canal in July. We flew from Amsterdam to Geneva for consultation with the World Health Organization to see if Shippy would return to his work in Egypt during this troubled time. The decision was made: We would return to Egypt.

As we soared into the air on our way to the Middle East once again, we did not anticipate the crisis awaiting us. Little did we know that we would be returning to Geneva in an unexpected way, and much sooner than we had ever dreamed!

11

The Suez Crisis

We landed at the Cairo Airport and went on to Maadi, where Shafik was waiting for us. We had a happy reunion with him and friends, and life seemed much as we had left it. I resumed my French lessons with Madame Drosso, which I enjoyed. The boys started school, and September passed quickly. We all adjusted easily back to our life in Egypt.

However, that quiet life was to be shattered unexpectedly in October. Gamal Adul Nasser, the president of Egypt, nationalized the Suez Canal. In response, Israel, Britain, and France prepared to attack Egypt to safeguard their interests in this vital waterway. On October 30, I was having my French lesson when the message came from the American Embassy to prepare at once for evacuation. Every embassy overseas has a notification and evacuation plan to remove their employees and U.S. citizens from danger zones, but the ultimate decision to stay or go lies with the individual citizens. The World Health Organization had its own policies, and the boys and I were ordered to evacuate while Shippy was to remain in Egypt. Three ships from the U.S. Sixth Fleet had been sent to the port of Alexandria, where they would evacuate those U.S. citizens and other foreign nationals who wished to leave. We were to drive by car in a convoy the following day (Shippy would accompany us to Alexandria) with one suitcase each to board the USS *Chilton*, an attack transport ship designed to carry troops for amphibious assaults.

After a busy and tense night we were packed and ready to join the convoy. Shafik packed us a lunch, and a friend drove a vehicle from Shippy's project that we would use for our trip. Around 2:00 P.M., we joined the convoy and inched our way toward Alexandria, finally arriving around 8:00 P.M. We spent the night in a hotel and then proceeded to the docks the next morning, where we lined up, family by family, to board the small boats that would take us to the USS *Chilton*. We said a difficult farewell to Shippy at the dock and then boarded the small "Mike" boats.

The trip out to the ship was uneventful until we arrived alongside. I took one look at the side of the ship where a long ladder extended almost vertically from the side of the main deck down to the water. We would have to scale these heights to board the ship! The boys clambered up first with the greatest of ease. I decided if I had any faith at all I would have to pray for help to get me to that top deck! I felt a surge of energy and went up that ladder like a gazelle! I give all credit to a higher power and younger legs! At the top was a big poster: "We knew you were coming, so we baked a cake." And we all ate navy cake!

The spirit on the ship was joyful and invigorating. People helped each other, and those with small babies were given special assistance. The captain and crew of the USS *Chilton* and the Navy's Sixth Fleet took great care of us, even giving up their Thanksgiving dinners to feed us. They will remain my heroes forever!

Because of the crowding on the ship and its design (to carry troops, not families), only the youngest children could remain with their parents. Consequently, Bruce and Richard berthed in another compartment of the ship, organized with other children as "junior Marines" supervised by real

Marines. As for me, I was assigned the top bunk in another compartment, as I had shown by the workout on the ladder that I could make it up there in my slip and pantyhose.

By the next day, we were all on board and ready to leave. We were ordered out on deck in life jackets as we left the harbor, with the minesweeper going before us. I took one last lingering look at the harbor as we slowly moved away. Hazy thoughts wandered through my mind. *When would I see Shippy again? Where were my boys on the ship right now? Where were we going? Would I ever see Egypt again?*

What did I have as I stood there on the deck of the *Chilton?* There were people all around me, but my sons were elsewhere on the ship, my husband was in Alexandria, and most of my worldly goods were left behind in Cairo. I do not wish to be overly dramatic, because this was a minor crisis compared to the devastating experiences of many today with floods, hurricanes, wars, and killing in so many areas of the world. Also, we were going out of Alexandria through possibly mined waters, but a minesweeper was sailing ahead of us. The issue was, what did I have within me to steady me to meet even a minor crisis?

I had one thing—Jesus. Where was my heart? In reading my Bible, I had learned from the words of Jesus Himself in Matthew 6:19–21, "Do not lay up for yourselves treasures on earth where moth and rust destroy and where thieves break in and steal. But lay up for yourselves treasures in Heaven where neither moth nor rust destroy and where thieves do not break in and steal. For where your treasure is, there your heart will be also," (KJV). Was my heart with Jesus?

And then I remembered in Matthew 8:24, where Jesus said, "Therefore whoever hears these sayings of mine, and does them, I will liken him to a man who built his house on a rock. And the rain descended, the floods came and the winds blew and beat on that house, and it did not fall for it was founded on a rock." In my Quest, I was finding Jesus now as my *rock*. From just a *name*, He became a *friend*, *helper*, and *master*. He was now my *rock,* telling me, "I will never leave you nor forsake you. Trust Me."

We sailed safely out of the harbor, shed our life jackets, and relaxed. The three ships of the evacuation force sailed for Souda Bay, Crete, where, because of the overcrowding on the *Chilton*, we were scheduled to transfer to another ship, the *Alexander Patch*, which was designed to transport large numbers of people. The *Patch* would then take us to Naples, Italy, for disembarkation.

The evening was passing when I saw a friend coming toward me with a big smile on her face and an air of excitement about her.

"Lois," she said. "Have your heard the news?"

"What news?" I responded.

"Your husband was ordered out at the last minute, and he is on the ship behind us. They just signaled the news from the USS *Thuban!*"

My heart leaped with a surge of joy! As the news spread around the ship, I felt that everyone was rejoicing with me—and they were!

When we reached Crete, the announcement came that we were to be ferried ashore in family units. Finally, our names were called: Lois Shipman, Bruce Shipman, Richard Shipman. Lois was there, Bruce appeared from the junior Marines, but no Richard. I had read about "Mother instinct," but at that moment I experienced it.

I turned to Bruce, "Where is your brother?"

"I don't know."

I turned to the officer directing us and said, "Where is my other son? I will not step into that boat without him."

He replied patiently and politely, "Don't be concerned, Mrs. Shipman. He's with the junior Marines and he will be taken off the ship with them.

"Don't worry," he repeated as he took my arm and decisively helped me into the boat.

To step into that boat without Richard was an emotional struggle that took every bit of self-control I had and some that I didn't have. The *Rock* within me and the small edge of mind-over-emotion enabled me to do it. To this day, it was one of the most difficult directions I have had to obey, even though there was no real danger to my son. I shall always respect the depth of Mother instinct!

We had a happy reunion with Shippy at Crete, and Richard did emerge safely with the junior Marines. The *Alexander Patch* sailed for Naples with our family safe and intact. The evacuation had been a disciplined, organized, and smooth operation. I was proud of our navy and proud to be an American. From then on I have been gung ho for the navy. Interestingly, Richard went on to become a naval aviator and served on the aircraft carriers *John F. Kennedy* and *Forrestal*. I especially treasure the small gold navy wings that he gave me.

My evacuation from Egypt was my first introduction to the U.S. Navy Sixth Fleet. As we sailed out of Egyptian waters on the USS *Chilton* with the minesweepers before us, I took the Sixth Fleet into my heart. They have remained there for forty-six years as I sail into the new millennium with them.

That day, long ago in October 1956, the navy exemplified for me one of many parts of our country that maintain and project the ideals upon which America was founded. It took into its protective care not only the Americans wishing to evacuate, but everyone of all races and nationalities wishing to be delivered out of harm's way. They did it with grace, style, skill, and even humor as our tension eased when we saw the huge cake they had baked for us.

Our trip from Crete to Naples was uneventful, and as we disembarked, we were met by the Red Cross with welcome coffee and doughnuts. World Health Organization officials were also present to coordinate our subsequent travel arrangements. We took a bus to Rome, where we stayed the night at a hotel not far from the Spanish Steps. The following day we traveled by train to Geneva, Switzerland, the headquarters of WHO, where we would live until it was safe to return to Egypt.

Suez wasn't the only world crisis occurring during this fall of 1956. Hungary revolted against Russia, resulting in a Russian invasion. Shippy was assigned to work with the many Hungarian refugees who were fleeing across the border. He was able to stay with us long enough to help us get settled into a furnished apartment on Rue de Lyon in Geneva. He left shortly thereafter, and the boys and I settled in for an unknown duration.

I held onto my *Rock* in this new world where life had picked me up and set me down again, like that leaf in a storm. However, I could think of few places lovelier than Geneva for the good Lord to have chosen.

12

Geneva, Switzerland, and Return to Egypt

Shippy had left Egypt so unexpectedly that he did not have even one suitcase. He departed for his work with the Hungarian refugees clothed in apparel borrowed or bought anew. Delving into our suitcases, the boys and I found a strange assortment. Richard had insisted on taking—a set of his favorite books with an odd mix of clothes interspersed among them. Bruce had a well selected collection of wearing apparel, albeit the majority of it suitable for a milder climate than that of Geneva. I found among my otherwise quite sensible collection a lace tablecloth and my sterling silver, along with some precious photographs. I must have thought that if I lost all my material possessions in Egypt, I could at least set a nice table wherever I was! An Austrian friend who evacuated with us found a bag of salt in her luggage. On asking her why she had included that strange item she replied, "I haven't the faintest idea!"

Our apartment was comfortable, and we felt very fortunate to have found it. The next important task was to find schools for the boys. At first they attended an emergency school set up at a local church for the families who had evacuated. However, when it became apparent that return to Egypt was not imminent, they entered the well established International School of Geneva.

The World Health people were supportive and helped us feel welcome in our new home. I was far from fluent in French, but what I did know was helpful in the shops around us on the Rue de Lyon. We bought bicycles for the boys so they could get around town and to school on the well laid-out network of bicycle lanes in Geneva. They made frequent trips to the airport, watching the numerous airplanes landing and taking off to unknown destinations. This was perhaps a formative experience for Richard, as he later went on to become an airline pilot.

Each Sunday we attended the American Church and afterward had dinner at a restaurant that specialized in steaks. I can truthfully say it was the best steak I have ever eaten. That Sunday dinner was always a gala occasion for us.

Shippy returned for Christmas, carrying gifts for all of us. We had a joyous holiday. We found a majestic Swiss Christmas tree, and the boys and I shopped with enthusiasm for sparkling decorations and lights to embellish it. The holiday season was embraced by all of us like a long-lost friend, made more precious by what we had gone through in previous months and our opportunity to be together as a family. We shared Christmas dinner with an older couple who had evacuated with us. The stars shone bright over Rue de Lyon as we rejoiced that Christmas night.

Alas, Shippy's return was brief. Once again we had to say good-bye, as he had been ordered by the WHO to return to Egypt. The U.S. Government, however, would not allow the families to return until the situation in Egypt became more stable. He left in January, and life went on for the boys and me as usual.

In later years, when I saw the movie *Casablanca,* I empathized with the refugees who were there during World War II as they looked wistfully into the sky at those fortunate enough to have visas flew away to freedom. With lingering longing, I also gazed into the sky from my kitchen window as the planes one by one left the Geneva Airport, wondering when the boys and I would be able to return to Egypt and Shippy. Geneva was certainly not captivity, but neither was it home nor were we together as a family.

In mid-April that longing was answered. The ban was lifted, and we could return! That is, Richard and I returned, but Bruce remained in Geneva. He was in his sophomore year at the International School and liked it very much, and we were reluctant to disrupt his education by leaving before the end of the school year. He was speaking French well and could stay at a family pension where we all had resided at one time, so he would not be in strange surroundings.

The departure day came, and Richard and I boarded the plane with exhilaration and anticipation. We were not disappointed! We were the only ones traveling first class. (We did not always travel first class and why this time we did I can't remember. I do remember that we thoroughly enjoyed it!) There were pink linen place mats, real china, delicious food served in three courses, and attentive service. After dessert, we were served Swiss chocolate Easter eggs as it was Easter eve. *C'est magnifique!* We stopped in Athens, Greece, where Richard and I walked around the airport to stretch our legs, and then on to Cairo. The airline also provided food at the airport, as if we needed it!

The airport at Cairo was now repaired after being bombed during the Suez War (which prevented us from evacuating by air, the original Embassy plan). Richard and I stepped off the plane to meet Shippy with joy. We drove directly to Maadi, where Shafik was waiting to greet us. He had stayed in our apartment and protected it and was there when Shippy returned in January. Not everyone was as fortunate. The servant of the couple in the apartment below us had sold all their furniture! Once again, I lifted up a thankful heart.

The atmosphere in Maadi was subdued, with one house after another standing vacant. Our Egyptian friends welcomed us back, and the people were happy to see the beginning of the return to normal life. Because of the exodus of many families, there were desirable houses to rent, and we went house-hunting. It was time to leave our high-rise apartment.

After a brief search, we found a two-story house with a huge garden. The dining room had French doors that opened onto a large terrace overlooking the garden, which had paths for leisurely strolling, complete with a charming pool with water lilies and various statues of interesting origin as to sculpture, stone, and workmanship. Throughout the garden were a profusion of riotous colors from every imaginable variety of flowers that only an uninhibited gardener might conceive. The total effect was awesome. We rented the house at once.

One detail I found out later about the house was its proximity to a Mosque. Every morning I was awakened by the haunting call to prayer that was an integral part of the Muslem worship. It was also a precious reminder to me to start the day with my Lord.

We moved in at once. Shippy was back at the project, the school was rejuvenated, and Richard returned to class, much happier than he had been in the Geneva school. Life slowly returned to its normal routine. But even though the crisis had been quickly brought to an end, there was suffering for the Egyptian people and hardship for all those involved. Before boarding the USS *Chilton*, I saw a plane brought down by Egyptian antiaircraft fire. English, French, Israeli, Egyptian—all suffered, and many were still enduring hardship and disrupted lives.

We had a number of visitors as life became more settled. Most were interested in visiting the village where the WHO team and Shippy were working. They were a brilliant and dedicated group of men and women, all invaluable in one field or another, working together out of concern for the health of the local people. It was a pleasure to know them and entertain them.

Shafik also was delighted to entertain our guests. He had a new galabia that was truly elegant. As the majordomo to his underlings, he ordered them about with great finesse. His reputation was at stake, and he was determined that each dinner would be perfect, to say nothing of the house itself. Every piece of silver and brass was polished until it not only shone, it dazzled. I tiptoed around, not daring to touch anything. I shared with him the menu and table decorations I had in my mind, and that was that! I then retired to be hostess at the appointed time. The dinner parties were a great success, and I'm sure Shafik's reputation reached a new high among his friends and coworkers.

Egypt was a land of contrast in many ways: pockets of wealth like Maadi surrounded by much poverty, vast deserts broken by the incredible fertility of the Nile Valley; cloudless blue skies obscured occasionally by sandstorms and locust swarms. Yes, that's right—locust swarms.

I had read about the locust in the Bible but never dreamed of ever seeing one. I was watching a tennis match one afternoon at the Maadi club, and suddenly the sky seemed to darken. People started to leave, and I looked up to see a huge cloud of locusts descending upon us, as many falling out of the sky as were flying over. I was wearing a low-neck summer dress, so I clasped my arms across my neck and ran for home. I reached safety and shut the door behind me. In due time, I'm not sure how long, the locusts passed and the sun returned. Shafik then wielded a broom with fervor and swept all the bodies off the terrace and surrounding areas. I sank into a chair, greatly relieved, and once again wondered what I would do without Shafik! I never expected locusts.

After the locusts passed, I reflected on the Biblical passages I had read about locusts. Joel 2:25 said, "So I will restore to you the years that the swarming locust has eaten" (KJV). This has always been comforting verse to me. As a young mother with my first child, my life had been normal and not touched to a great extent by the war. I had time to spend with my baby and enjoy him. With Richard, the pressures of war did engulf me, and although there were many happy times, the leisure just to enjoy his baby days was limited. That is why I love this verse from Joel. The "locusts of war" robbed me of the full, leisurely enjoyment of my second baby, but the Lord has restored to me those years that they had "eaten." Due to life's circumstances, I have been able to see Richard often in later years and share vacations at Hilton Head Island. The ties with Bruce were also close as I traveled with him during his school years in England.

The days in Egypt were slipping by and we savored them to the utmost. Perhaps we sensed that our days in Egypt were coming to an end. In the spring of 1958, Shippy was appointed to be Chief Sanitary Engineer for the Pan American Health Organization (PAHO), headquartered in Washington, D.C. We would be leaving in May.

Life then took on an impetus, and we were caught up in final preparations to leave. There were, of course, the farewell parties and good-byes. Our furniture was put up for auction, and packing began in earnest. The day before we left, I took one last walk in my garden and sat for some time by the lily pond. We had been given these years abroad, together as a family. They were a precious gift. Before too long the boys would be in college, preparing for a life of their own. That is as it should be, but I realized life would be very different for me m Washington, D.C. Again it would be a challenge but also a great opportunity to learn and grow in a city of history, culture, and beauty.

On the last day in my beautiful garden, I said, "Good-bye, Egypt." The years there I will never forget, with precious memories stored in my mind and my heart. From time to time I will venture into my precious storehouse and bring the memories out one by one: the palm trees along the Nile, the flame trees aglow, the poinsettias in our garden at Christmas, Shafik in his galabia, the tombs in the Valley of the Kings, drifting down the Nile in a felucca, square dancing on the roof the yacht club, our picnics at the pyramids, dining and dancing on the roof of the old Semiramis Hotel, the little church in Maadi, waking in the morning to the call to prayer from the mosque nearby, our wedding anniversary with the boys at the Mena House in the shadow of the Great Pyramids, Shippy's coworkers and the village, Yousef and his family, and there are so many others.

I will take each one out and dust it off and handle it carefully and then gently put it back into my storehouse and go about my business. But, quoting Wordsworth, they will always be there "to flash upon that inward eye, which is the bliss of solitude," and then, "my heart with pleasure fills" as I remember the wonder and beauty that is Egypt.

The last and most difficult good-bye was to Shafik. My future was secure; his was not. He was a Coptic Christian, my brother in Christ. I wished him well and said, "God willing, may we meet again some day."

"Inshallah," he said.

"Inshallah," I replied.

13

Return Home

Our first stop on our homeward journey was the World's Fair in Brussels, Belgium. We toured the fairgrounds, admiring the stunning buildings and exhibits, including the outstanding United States exhibition. In the evening, the boys returned to the fairgrounds while Shippy and I attended the ballet where Margot Fonteyn was dancing the *Firebird*. This performance was a special treat for me as I am an aficionado of the ballet.

From Brussels we flew to Geneva for Shippy's last goodbye to his chief and friends in the Middle East region of the World Health Organization. From this point, our travel plans back home had been carefully worked out by Bruce, our travel expert, and they were excellent.

From Switzerland we flew to Denmark and spent some time in Copenhagen. We filled the days with sightseeing in this cosmopolitan city that fascinated us in our different areas of interest and knowledge. We visited the delightful Tivoli Gardens and then proceeded to Elsinore Castle, devouring Danish pastries along the way. Bruce was especially impressed with this castle made famous by Hamlet.

Bergen, Norway, was our next destination. We were surprised when we had to draw heavy velvet curtains in our hotel room to keep out the light so we could sleep—at midnight! The Norwegian countryside was spectacular, particularly the many fjords. These narrow arms of the seas jutted inland and were surrounded by steep cliffs, providing beautiful vistas from the small ships that sailed them. Bruce, in searching through his many travel books, had found an attractive place to stay in Ulvik on the Hardanger Fjord. After a scenic boat ride up the fjord, we settled happily into our hotel, where we spent four days that are in the pure golden section of my memory. The view surrounding us had a beauty and grandeur that reduced one to silence. I felt a sense of awe at the majesty in the scenes before me. Always I will appreciate the glorious mountains in Switzerland and the profusion of flowers that seemed to flourish everywhere, but this was different. It was an austere beauty that demanded a hushed obeisance in the presence of its magnificence. Psalm 19 came to mind, "The Heavens declare the glory of God, and the firmament showeth forth His handiwork."

With wonder and reverence, the thought came to me that this was a perfect revelation of God that I was beholding. No wonder I felt that I should kneel in its presence.

From the sublime to the earthy, at dinner one evening we were served reindeer as our main course. This was a new experience for all of us. Bruce and Shippy, ever the eager gourmets, "fell to" with gusto. Richard and I were more tentative. However, we eventually took the plunge and found it very tasty.

On our final day, Shippy and the boys went fishing in the icy cold waters of the fjord, while I wandered by myself, lost in the scenic delights around me. I yearned that time would stand still, but unfortunately, it does not.

Our sailing date was approaching, and the time came when we had to leave by train for Goteborg, Sweden. From there we were to sail home on the new Swedish liner, the *Gripsholm*. We boarded this sparkling, new ship with a sense of excitement and anticipation. Sailing out of the harbor we were engulfed in good-bye waves and cheers, with confetti cascading around us.

I stood by the railing watching the harbor grow dim in the distance and finally drifting out of my sight. I thought, poignantly, as I could see it no longer, thus in like manner, the life I had lived these past years abroad was disappearing also.

This would be our fourth and last crossing together as a family. These years abroad had been happy ones. I lifted up a grateful heart; I would never take them for granted. I knew they had been a gift to me and that I had been especially blessed. I also knew there would be challenges ahead for all of us, not only myself.

Separation would come, as the boys would eventually leave for college. Hopefully, for all of us, there would be growth in the Lord. I especially longed to know Jesus more intimately. I prayed that somehow, somewhere, He could use me to bring His blessing and salvation to others.

I walked slowly to our cabin, still deep in contemplation. I made a promise to myself that the first thing I would do when I was settled in the nation's capital was to ask Jesus for a prayer partner. A deep sense of peace settled upon me. It was going to be a good crossing.

That sense of peace was well founded. I was given not only one prayer partner in answer to my plea, but two! Gwen and Marie were about to enter my life in Washington, D.C.

Each day was filled to overflowing on our ship, with many activities planned for our enjoyment. A charming group of Swedish dancers performed folk dances on deck each day, which I especially appreciated. Of course, there was tempting food available day and night. I forgot my waistline completely! At times, my memory echoes the sound of the foghorns as we encountered some reduced visibility sailing through the North Sea. It was a soft, reassuring sound, not a frightening one to me.

The Captain's dinner was a great success! There were large creations made of ice, which adorned a center table, each one designed with beauty and creativity. I felt festive and aglow in my lovely red dress and flowers in my hair with Shippy, handsome in his tuxedo, by my side. The waiters were in fine form and served us with great panache. As frosting on the cake, the boys were there to enjoy it with us.

It was a night to remember. I wished that it would never end. At long last, having danced until the wee hours, we had to accept the inevitable and say good night, while the orchestra played the final song, "I'll See You in My Dreams." We walked to our cabin with the soft strains of the music following us.

The next day we were packed and on deck as we stood together watching with mixed emotions for the Statue of Liberty to come into view. At last she was here, lifting her torch to welcome us home. We disembarked and walked the streets of New York once again.

The Innocents had returned, not quite so innocent now!

Part Three: Back in the U.S.: The Quest Continues

14

Settling In and the Inner City

As usual, our first priority on arriving in Washington, D.C., was to find a place to live. Shippy was inundated with conferences and adjustments in his new position, so finding suitable living quarters was my responsibility. Bruce and Richard joined me, and together we started our search. School would be starting soon, so it was imperative that we find a house without undue delay. With a friendly real estate agent at our side, we began. After a week of intensive inspection of house after house, we narrowed the choice to two in the Chevy Chase area of Maryland. Neither Bruce, Richard, nor I could decide which was the right one for us. Shippy took one look at them both and then informed me that the final decision was mine! Bruce and Richard were neutral. As you can guess by now, I sank weakly into a chair and told the Lord I didn't have a clue which was the best choice. I asked Him to somehow lead me to the right decision, as it was an important one for all of us. I remembered what had been branded on my heart, "In all your ways acknowledge Him, and He will direct your paths," (Prov. 3:6).

Okay, Lord, I'm asking You to direct my path. Thank You for Your answer, I prayed.

The decision was made to look at both houses one last time, the next evening. Bruce, Richard, and I trudged over the same paths again to house number one. I was as confused as ever. With the real estate agent patiently following us, we climbed up the steps of house number two. As I was doing so, a deep sense of peace and also a feeling of oneness with the surroundings came over me. "We will buy it," I said, making sure Bruce and Richard were in accord.

To be absolutely honest, I must add a few words on the aftermath of my decision. The next day when the sober details of buying a house (and the cost!) and the full realization of my responsibility in choosing it dawned on me in the light of a new day, I felt somewhat shaken. What had I done! Was it really the right choice? The real estate agent could see I was a bit worried and said with assurance, "Mrs. Shipman, it is a lovely home, and you have made a good choice." Then a still, small thought came into my mind, "Where is your faith? Shame on you!"

The real estate agent's words indeed proved to be true. The house on Edgevale Street in Chevy Chase, Maryland, served us well. We lived there, happily, for over thirty years. As an added bonus, I received a lovely bouquet of flowers from the real estate agent, a gesture to help assuage my anxiety crisis, no doubt.

After settling into our new home, I remembered the promise I had made to myself and prayed for a prayer partner. It was an entirely new life that was unfolding before me once again, and I needed deeper resources to meet the challenges I would encounter here in the nation's capital. In answer to my prayers, I met two young mothers at the nearby church we attended. As I grew to know them better, I felt a bond with each of them. This affinity gave me the courage to ask if they would be interested in a Bible study in my home each Monday morning. One friend replied that she would be willing to try it for six weeks, and the other agreed to do likewise. We started in the sunroom of my home and met faithfully for over twenty-five years. The Lord had answered my prayer. He gave me not one, but two prayer partners, and, as the Bible promises, "good measure, pressed down and running over!" (Luke 6:38). Gwen and Marie had been sent into my life.

When I say, "we met faithfully," I truly mean it. After sitting in the same place each week for a number of years, we wore the carpet threadbare! In due time, we had to buy a new one. It was a beautiful carpet, and I'm still enjoying it today in my condo in Connecticut.

We had no teacher except the Lord Himself. Somehow, in addition to the Bible, just the right books found their way into our hands. In reading the book of James, we pondered on God's words, "Thus also faith by itself, if it does not have works, is dead" (James 2:17 ?). In time, after prayer, it was decided that we needed to reach out and touch others in need, in addition to our study of God's Word and our inspirational reading. However, we knew from our study two great truths: (1) "Unless the Lord builds the House, they labor in vain who built it. . ." (Psalm 127:1). We knew we would have to undergird any work we might do with prayer, and seek God's direction; (2) "And now abideth faith, hope, love, these three; but the greatest of these is love" (1 Corinthians 13:13).

We also knew that if we didn't love the people to whom we were reaching out, we would "labor in vain." Only Jesus could give us that love, and we must trust Him to do so. Undergirded by these truths, we started to work with a caseworker in the Aid to Dependent Mothers program of the Department of Human Resources in the District of Columbia. The caseworker would choose a family whose mother and children, hopefully, would accept us as friends. And so we began.

We worked for over twenty years and had the privilege to know and love three families in the inner city. We became like three great-aunts, visiting them and taking the children out on excursions in the parks around D.C. and Maryland, touring the museums on the Mall, visiting on holidays laden with specially chosen gifts and food we had prepared with such joy. They accepted us, and we accepted them in simple love and friendship.

There was sadness along with the joy, especially in our second "adopted" family. We grieved when we lost two of our boys, Timothy and Jay Carl, one to AIDS and the other to an overdose of drugs and alcohol. Timothy was a gifted boy, and we had sent him and his younger brother, Jay Carl, to YMCA Camp Letts in the hope of expanding their horizons and perhaps opening doors for growth and opportunities outside of their limited environment. Timothy loved plants and flowers, and we saw him off to Camp Letts carrying one of his most precious specimens. He also liked to sew, and we bought him a used sewing machine. He made curtains and other embellishments for their apartment during his school years. He did well in school, and on graduation found work in a bank. He told us at a young age that his dream was to work in a bank and wear a white shirt and tie. His dream came true, but at age thirty-one, he died of AIDS.

Shippy and I attended his funeral. We grieved with his family and friends, as did Gwen, Marie, and I . Could we have done more?

I grieve again as I write this for the mother, with whom I kept in touch until she died recently. She had sent me the death certificate of the younger boy, Jay Carl, who died from an overdose of drugs and alcohol after I left Maryland in later years. The last time I had seen him was with his mother at Shippy's memorial service at Chevy Chase Methodist Church. Gwen, Marie, and I laid both the boys to rest, but they are still alive for us as we share our memories of our times together with them.

However, the story and our experiences were not always sad. In our first "adopted" family there were many happy times. We are still in touch with them, especially the two elder daughters. Unexpectedly, one of the daughters called me just as I was writing about them. Dear Sheila! It was a happy surprise.

She said with a laugh, "We were all thinking about you three and remembering the fun times we had together, so just decided to call you!" She is doing well in an executive position of responsibility in the inner city. The elder sister is a teacher of many years in the D.C. school system. Her daughter is now attending an excellent college in Maryland. Mrs. C., their mother, is alive and well and is a friend we admire and love.

The third "adopted" family we also remember with affection and hear from, especially at Christmas. One of the daughters in this family is also at college. We helped them celebrate when they moved into a new house, which was a gala occasion. I recall we had a picnic on the Mall with the children and visited the Air and Space Museum and Natural History Museum. We shared the thrill of locating the Hope Diamond as we stood transfixed before its beauty!

After twenty years, it was becoming more difficult for us to go into the inner city, for various reasons. The children in our own families were growing up, and Gwen and I were traveling a great deal. Our visits grew fewer, but we never lost touch with the "adopted" families, and we miss them. However, to reach out to a fourth family was not "written," as they say in the Middle East.

Often I have thought of former President Bush's speech on the "Thousand Points of Light" that bless and strengthen our nation. Our experiences in the inner city blessed and strengthened us. The friendships with our three families will always be "points of light" that will illumine our lives forever.

Another "point of light" for me during this period was a first time meeting with Gwen's niece, Vicki, who was visiting for a short time from England. She was seeking purpose and direction in her life, and I felt a loving empathy with her.

After she returned home, during my quiet time with the Lord, I "listened" for any words of encouragement and help the Lord might have for her. The thoughts flowed as I wrote them down in my notebook. They were "points of light" for me as well as for Vicki, and I felt led to write Vicki. As I read and re-read that letter, I felt bound to Vicki with ties of Jesus' eternal love. His light shines on me as well as on her as we are one in Him. Here are the thoughts that came to me for her during my quiet time with the Lord. They were the truth and guidelines for me, also, in my own Quest.

"Dear Vicki, stay close to Me, your Master. Walk hand in hand with Me and let Me and Me alone have full authority over your life. Look neither left nor right but UP TO ME, and let the light of My countenance shine down upon you and perfect that which concerneth you and conform you to My image.

As you walk close to Me, My light will penetrate every part of your being, and truth and joy and love with flow from Me to you. Let me search you for that which is displeasing in My sight and pray for conviction of sins and the gift of repentance.

But the path is straight and the way is narrow into my Kingdom, and I have told you that 'I am the *way*, the *truth* and the *light*.' Only by following Me and My Word with you find your way into my land. 'Where your eye is single, then is your body full of light.' Keep your eye on Me alone, and look only to Me for guidance and direction and decisions. *Each morning as the dawn breaks and a new day opens before you, look to Me for direction and the plan for that day and give yourself to Me to use as I wish. Let your single eye gravitate to Me as a needle of a compass, and I will surely be your God and you will be My child.*

You will be loved and cared for and directed and fulfilled and used by Me for My Divine Purposes. I will fill you with My peace, My joy, My unselfish love, and I will deliver you from sin and evil and give you My power within to draw others to Me. *Stay near, dearest Vicki! Hold My hand as you go through each day; talk to Me and walk with Me and I will be your beloved companion.* Read My word faithfully and obey My commands with the strength and power I give you within. My arms are around you; My hand of blessing has been laid on your head. Put on My protective armor and face the world, the flesh and the devil encompassed in My Divine Protection. All love to you from your Savior, Jesus Christ, who died and suffered on the cross for you, My Vicki, My child. Amen, Amen."

15

PAHO and the Empty Nest

Shippy was now chief engineer for the Pan American Health Association (PAHO), the branch of the World Health Organization focused on North and South America. He did not speak Spanish, however, so after the housing situation was settled, we both started taking lessons at the high school nearby. I was happy to refresh my skills, as I had studied Spanish for two years at the University of Minnesota. While he was learning, Shippy was ably assisted in his work by a dedicated Latin American secretary who helped him immeasurably with the correspondence and paperwork. He also started to travel extensively in Latin America, visiting water projects in the various countries.

I also became acquainted with the wives of other PAHO personnel, our new compatriots. I entertained a great deal at this time (sadly without Shafik, I might add). The Latin women charmed me completely with their warmth, friendliness, and encouragement of my halting Spanish.

At the end of our first year in Washington, another crisis was approaching for me. I had envisioned it as we sailed out of the Swedish harbor on our way home. Bruce had finished his senior year of high school, and the time had come for him to leave for college. The "empty nest" was starting to become a reality. Bruce was accepted at Carleton College, a liberal arts school in Northfield, Minnesota. We had visited the school during the summer months and found it impressive. I said good-bye to him in the fall, with a hug and a tear. As I passed by his empty room that first evening, I decided I must start to re-feather my nest. I did not know what to do or where to start in this venture. But the Lord knew.

Within a year or so, a lady at my church, who I did not know, approached me. She told me she had heard that my elder son was away at college and that I had another son who was a student at the Bethesda Chevy Chase High School. When I replied that this was true, she asked me if I would consider taking a teenage Cuban boy into our home for a year while he attended his senior year in high school. Nick had been in the mountains of Cuba with Fidel Castro but at some point had experienced a Christian conversion. The Methodist Church was sponsoring him in his quest to become an ordained minister, with the first step being his completion of high school. I told her we would discuss it as a family and let her know. We did, and agreed to welcome Nick into our home for his senior year. The yellow room (Bruce's bedroom) was to be occupied again. The nest would once more have two occupants.

As I look back at that year, I am truly amazed how easy it was to adjust to this change that we all experienced. Nick himself was the key. He admired Shippy and respected him. Never once did he refuse to obey the rules we had set for Richard that we applied to him as well. Richard was tentative with his acceptance but friendly with a wait-and-see attitude. I think he was a bit wary that Nick would outshine him scholastically. (He need not have worried about that!) For myself, I found his background interesting, to say the least, but I thought it best to live one day at a time and take if from there.

As time progressed, we grew into a real family. Richard and Nick became good friends, and Nick was part of us. There were some interesting sidelights beyond school and study. We learned in a short time that the girls were quite interested in Nick. He came home one afternoon with a cage and a mouse that one of his admiring girl friends had given to him. I have already stated my feelings about mice! I fussed a bit, but as long as it was in the cage, I didn't mind so much. However, as I'm sure you can guess, somehow the mouse escaped, and no one could catch it. Its one redeeming feature was that it was white with pink eyes. As the days went by, my nerves were becoming increasingly jangled. I would sit down for a short afternoon or evening rest, and there it would appear in the room, unexpectedly. It would fix its beady eyes on me and then scampered off. I have to confess, I tried to set a trap, but the sight of that pink-and-white creature over the days had started a relationship. I couldn't kill it! *What to do? What to do?* The answer came with athletic Richard. Once, when an uninvited bat found its way into the sunroom, he was able to divert it out the door with judicious swipes of his tennis racquet. So the next time I saw the little creature that I knew for certain was bent on harassing me, I yelled to him for help. Richard came on the run with a broom and was able to sweep my white-and-pink antagonist out the door as it scampered by.

The year passed with no major crisis, and Shippy and I proudly saw both Nick and Richard graduate from high school. Nick went on to seminary but did not complete his training. Eventually he moved to New Jersey, where his parents had settled when they emigrated to the United States. Nick came back to visit us twice, first with a friend and later with his wife and child. He showed his friend all around the house and told him what a happy year it had been. Yes, it had been—for everyone.

Again the empty nest was looming before me. Now both sons would be in college. We said good-bye to Richard in the fall of 1962 as he left for Macalester College in St. Paul,

Minnesota. There were more hugs and more tears, and I faced two empty rooms now, with Nick gone. However, the angels in heaven and the Lord Himself had not overlooked my plight. Out of the past, Julie reappeared in our lives. She was a longtime friend of the family who had just returned from Turkey to study for a master's degree in linguistics at American University in Washington, D.C. She needed a place to stay! The Lord works in mysterious ways, His wonders to behold. My longed for "daughter" was appearing, albeit a little late, but at a perfect time in my life. It was to be a blissful year together.

Julie and her family had lived across the street from us when we first arrived in Egypt. Her father was an agriculturist with the Agency for International Development, and her mother was a homemaker. I was a friend of her mother and marveled at the delicious cakes she produced with such ease. (I don't think she ever had a cook!)

There were four children in their family, two boys and two girls. Bruce and the elder boy John became good friends as the months went by. Living across the street from one another, they devised a private communication system. From our third story balcony, they connected a long string running down to John's house. Exactly how they communicated using this string is unclear in my memory, but the secret communications gave great satisfaction and pleasure to the participants.

Julie was the eldest of the four children. She was a gifted teenager, both scholastically and musically. After graduating from high school in Cairo, she went back to the States for her college education but returned overseas to teach English as a second language in Turkey. When she arrived in Washington to start her master's program, she called us to say hello and to ask if we had any suggestions as to where she might stay during her school year.

She arrived like a dove from heaven at this auspicious time of two empty rooms in our house. We welcomed her with open arms! Thus began a year that we remember with great joy.

Bruce was in school at King's College in London, on his Junior year abroad from Carleton College. However, Richard returned home on holidays and summer breaks from Macalester College. He and Julie had a happy and interesting relationship. They were both athletic and competed in a game (if you can call it that) they called "jousting." Each would confront the other in a solid stance with their hands raised to their chest, palms up in a patty-cake position. The object of the game was to knock the other off balance by striking the hands only. This inevitably produced much arm flailing, as the participants struggled to maintain balance following a well struck blow. Aside from knocking over one lamp, denting a lampshade, and developing a few bruised egos (mostly on Richard's side), the jousting events produced no lasting damage and seemed to give much pleasure and satisfaction, particularly to the winner.

Richard was always ready to work and earn some extra money. Julie, in those days (it is quite different today), neither cooked nor ironed. She contracted a deal with Richard to iron her clothes for fifty cents per item. It proved to be a happy arrangement for them both and continued whenever Richard was home from school.

Julie and I survived two of her disappointing romances as the relationships disintegrated. We also survived a difficult-to-treat cut Julie inflicted upon herself opening a can. Julie is a tall girl, and I am on the short side. It was difficult to hold her upright and treat the flow of blood, as she would keep sagging in a near faint. We managed, though, and everything happily turned out all right.

Last, but not least, Julie wanted to entertain some of her classmates at American University and wanted to pay me for hosting the dinner. I said, "Fine, but I certainly don't expect any money."

But Julie is an independent minded young lady. "No," she said, "I insist on paying for each dinner."

So she hired me for so much per plate. I donned my apron, searched my cookbooks, and put on a good dinner (so she said). I enjoyed meeting her friends very much and had a great time. Nevertheless, a lingering thought of Shafik came to mind in the midst of the cleaning up.

On June 19, 1963, I attended Julie's graduation from American University, the only one of her "family" to be with her, as her real parents were abroad in Jordan. It was an impressive ceremony with President John F. Kennedy giving the commencement address, which was also a major foreign policy speech. The following November he was assassinated in Texas.

After the graduation ceremony, Julie and I returned to Bethesda and celebrated with an Orange Freeze at the popular Hot Shoppe. Julie went on to an excellent position with the U.S. Information Agency (USIA) in Washington, D.C., and was later granted admission to the prestigious National Press Club. In later years, she invited me to lunch with her there, which I thoroughly enjoyed. We are both hopeless romantics and we shared and sighed over our beloved years in Egypt.

Julie is now married to a distinguished astronomer she met at the USIA. They have a house in Culpeper, Virginia, as well as a farm in Virginia and an apartment in Washington, D.C.. We stay in close touch. No natural daughter could I cherish more than Julie.

16

Bruce and England

Bruce spent his junior year abroad at King's College in London, England. Shippy was in Pakistan on his work, and we planned to meet in London and fly home together to spend Christmas with Richard and Nick. This would also enable us to see Bruce during the holiday. I packed and flew alone to London to spend the week before Christmas with Bruce before Shippy flew in. Shippy and I felt that, as high school seniors, Richard and Nick could cope by themselves for one week.

This was my first visit to England, and I was excited and thrilled to see Bruce and to explore London. Bruce was living in a residence hall with a roommate, and I was put up in a guest quarters across the street. We started at once to see the sights of London.

I was dazzled by the Christmas decorations, especially on Regent Street. Lois was in "wonderland" once again! Arches over the street made a canopy of brilliant Christmas colors interspersed with an incredible number of lights reflecting and shading the sparkling arches. Silver ornaments scattered throughout shone like jewels in a Sultan's treasure chest.

I met Bruce's roommate and his friend Charles, who was singing in a concert of Christmas music that we were planning to attend. Bruce and I shared an evening of heavenly music (there is no other word for it) as the superb Choir of Kings College sang sacred Christmas music.

After the concert, Bruce decided I should see and dine at the famous old eating place, the Cheshire Cheese, where the great English writer Samuel Johnson gathered with his friends. We walked and we walked and we walked, but no Cheshire Cheese appeared. I was blissfully absorbing all the strange and different sights of London, unaware of the passing of time. Believe me, we did indeed cover a lot of ground!

We ended our trek finally at a trendy Italian restaurant, which due to our murmuring stomachs and weakening legs, seemed no less than manna sent to us from above. The Cheshire Cheese would have to wait until another time.

The following day, I visited every china shop I could find and bought teapots, teacups, and Liberty Department Store scarves for all my friends. That evening, Bruce and I went to Covent Garden to see the ballet *Sleeping Beauty*. The great ballerina, Margot Fonteyn, (who I had seen in Brussels) was dancing the role of Princess Aurore.

My biggest thrill was when Bruce took me to tea at Harrods, the famous English department store. He appeared in his navy blue blazer with the impressive crest of red and gold of King's College sewn on his pocket. I was so proud and happy that I continued to beam for sometime afterwards.

There is an interesting sequel to this story. In later years, Bruce was cleaning out his closets in preparation for a move. I was with him as he brought out an armful of clothes that he intended to donate to a nearby parish. All at once I spied The Blazer from King's College with The Crest! I grabbed it with both hands as if it were a living thing, hugged it in my arms, and proclaimed, "You can't give this away!" After a certain amount of cajoling and remonstrating, I finally agreed to the blazer donation if Bruce would cut the emblem from the pocket and give it to me. I was thinking ahead. I would have it sewn on a blazer I own (regardless of my age). My heart sang as I took possession of this precious heirloom and carefully secured it in my purse.

Shippy arrived at the end of the week, and the three of us had a day of intense sightseeing together. I have wished often that time could stand still, but it never cooperates with my wishes. Shippy and I had to say good-bye to Bruce. We were happy to find him completely settled into his new life and adjusting extremely well to his English environment.

Our flight left on schedule, but to my great surprise I discovered that Shippy had a first class ticket while I was flying coach. As it turns out, Shippy had coordinated with the World Bank to terminate his overseas work with a London-New York itinerary, meaning his business would pay the bill. I was on my own resources, however, hence the coach seat. Nevertheless, I worked very hard to keep a positive attitude. Shippy did come back once to my seat to say hello. Oh well, you can't have everything!

Bruce successfully finished his junior-year-abroad program and returned to Carleton College to complete his senior year. England was clearly in his blood, however. After graduating, he left again for England, this time to attend Oxford University to earn a degree in theology.

Shippy was away, Richard was in college, Nick and Julie were gone, so Bruce called from Oxford and suggested that I fly to England and spend his three-week spring break with him. He would work out an itinerary for us, and we could travel together, perhaps even going to Edinburgh by train. I did not need any encouragement. I flew out of Dulles

Airport, my spirits rising along with the aircraft as it lifted off for Heathrow Airport.

Bruce met me at the airport, and we left London by train for Oxford. There I settled into the Old Parsonage Guest House. The heating system in the old parsonage house was definitely as described in its name: old. I slept in my pajamas plus my robe and bedroom slippers, with my coat and a sweater thrown over the blanket. And this was in the spring! (This was many years ago, and I understand it is now warm and cozy.)

It would take more than a little chill to daunt my spirits, and the next morning I was excited and happy as Bruce escorted me around Oxford University. The grounds and gardens were lovely, the buildings dignified and hallowed by age. Magdalen College was magnificent, with even a deer gamboling on the green. The spires of the chapels and cathedrals impressed me, and the lawns and flowers flourished, reflecting meticulous care. We visited the Ashmolean Museum, where I especially enjoyed the Egyptian and Chinese exhibits. After seeing Bruce's room at St. Stephens House, we enjoyed tea at the Mitre Hotel and had dinner with a friend of the writer C. S. Lewis.

The following day, I checked out of the old parsonage and boarded a bus with Bruce to Woodstock and Blenheim Castle, where Winston Churchill was born. We walked around the extensive grounds, and I gazed with truly awestruck wonder at the vastness of both the grounds and the castle itself. On our tour of the castle, I was impressed by a large painting of the ninth Duke of Marlborough and his American wife, Consuela Vanderbilt, with their sons. My interest was both artistic and personal as I pondered on this young bride adjusting to her new life in these overpowering surroundings.

We enjoyed a two-hour bus ride through the Midlands, eventually arriving at Stratford and Shakespeare country. There we lingered for two days of sightseeing in this famous area. By train we traveled to Manchester, where we rented a car. We drove to the Devonshire Estate of Chatsworth and spent happy hours viewing its grandeur. We gave thanks for Bruce's driving (on the left side of the road) which, albeit a bit erratic, nonetheless delivered us safely to our destinations.

Bruce was a perfect traveling companion. He was full of zest and had a big laugh. In addition, he was a fount of knowledge on all manner of subjects. Moreover, he was ready to stop and eat often, all of which pleased me very much. We ate a hearty breakfast, then stopped for elevenses at the designated hour, had lunch a few hours later, tea at 4:00 P.M., and finally supper in the evening. I never felt so well, and I never gained any weight!

We left Manchester by bus and had an interesting five-hour drive to Keswick and the Lake country. It was April, and the daffodils were in full bloom. I remembered Wordsworth's poem about the daffodils: "When all at once I saw a crowd, a host of golden daffodils. Beside the lake, beneath the trees, fluttering and dancing in the breeze." As Wordsworth wrote long ago, Bruce and I beheld them, "ten thousand saw we at a glance, tossing their heads in sprightly dance. The waves beside them danced, but they outdid the sparkling waves in glee."

The daffodils are another of the precious memories I remove from my hidden storehouse from time to time to enjoy once again as "they toss their heads in sprightly dance."

From Manchester, we took a smooth, fast train to Carlisle, where we visited the cathedral and surrounding countryside. We then boarded another train and enjoyed a nice dinner as we skimmed along the bleak and vast hills of Scotland, headed for Edinburgh.

After a restful night in our hotel, we started a busy and full day, fortified by Scotch porridge (of course). Our first stop was St. Giles Cathedral, where we spent some time visiting (remember, Bruce was reading theology at Oxford). It was a lovely, old, and impressive building with beautiful windows. We then walked to the Old Castle and toured it diligently. By then we had done a considerable amount of walking so decided to have tea. We dined in a most unusual room in the tower of the castle, complete with an old, huge fireplace, which gave it a true medieval touch (I told you we ate often!)

Fortified by food and with our feet rested, we continued our walking tour with a visit to Holyrood House, where Mary Queen of Scots had resided, and then on to the art museum. I was developing a love for great art and was impressed by the quality and variety of masterpieces displayed. After more walking and sightseeing, we left for Haworth, home of the famous Bronte family, and the moors.

I had been reading a great deal about the Bronte family, and *Jane Eyre,* by Charlotte Bronte, is one of my favorite novels. I told Bruce that I would like to see the old Bronte parsonage where they lived and walk on the moors.

We hiked about four miles after visiting the old parsonage. It was a beautiful day, mild and sunny, and as we walked deeper into the heart of the moors, I began to understand how the Brontes could love them so much. They are unusual. Little can grow on them except heather, but the mauve and purple colors of the heather in the distance and all around us created an incredible and beautiful panorama.

The parsonage was well designed, nicely kept, and more livable that I had expected. My reading about the Bronte family gave me a background that helped me appreciate what I was seeing and experiencing. I found the tiny manuscripts of their early childhood writings especially interesting. As we left Haworth to catch the bus for York, I took one last backward look at the steep street they all had tread so often, awed by the genius and tragedy of the Brontes.

We took the express train to London from York and spent two days in sightseeing around that great city. Our last night we had colas in a lovely salon of our hotel and talked until midnight. Bruce's friend Charles surprised me at breakfast next morning with a "going home" rose. We checked out of the hotel and boarded a bus for the airport. It was hard to say good-bye, but the moment had to come. The flight was crowded, and there were people still in the aisles as I finally found my seat. I was not seeing very well as I brushed away a tear and thought of Bruce. This was the baby I had given to a Jesus who I did not even know those many years ago. He was now alive and well, studying theology at Oxford University. God is good.

I had a nice missionary lady from Japan sitting next to me. She talked continuously, so that helped to take my mind away from leaving Bruce. Shippy was waiting for me at the Washington Airport, having just returned from South America. It was spring in Washington, and all the trees and flowers were beginning to blossom. I gave him a big welcome hug and silently prayed, "Thank you, Lord, for the gift of the past three weeks. Now let me blossom here like the flowers around me in whatever You would have me do for You. May Your will be done in my years ahead."

17

The World Bank and around the World

After four years with PAHO, Shippy was recruited by the World Bank to be its first senior water supply engineer. We discussed the decision, and Shippy consulted a trusted friend in the World Health Organization. It was apparent that this new position would open broader fields for Shippy's work in environmental sanitation. He decided to accept, and I concurred.

The time inevitably came to say good-bye to our Latin American friends. There were many parties including an especially nice luncheon given by the PAHO wives for me. I pondered how I might best express my love and appreciation for their friendship. The thought came to me to write a farewell speech. This I did—but in Spanish! I spent a great deal of time and loving thought on writing this, as I wanted it to be just right in grammar and content.

The day came, and a lovely day it was as I gave my surprise speech in (they said) perfect Spanish. I knew deep in my heart this would please them more than anything I could say or do in English—and it did! They were delightful ladies, and I still miss them.

Shippy accepted the World Bank offer to broaden the scope of his career, and as always, my life was enlarged along with his. During Shippy's years with the Bank, I was fortunate to fly around the world twice with him as he traveled on his work. This was possible because of a much-appreciated plan the World Bank had worked out for the wives of the employees. Sensitive to the amount of travel demanded of its people, the Bank awarded the wives one point for each day their husbands were out of the country on Bank business. When they had accrued three hundred points, the wives could accompany their husbands on a trip of their choosing, at bank expense. I had two 300-point trips, so you can see I paid my dues in days alone—but it was worth it!

I could write at length about the experiences we had on those two trips around the world, but I will mention only two. Both involved faith and a measure of self-control.

The first incident occurred just as we had finished a delightful few days in Hong Kong, approximately midway in our first trip. We were packed and ready to leave the elegant Peninsula Hotel (one of my favorite places to stay). Since we were early, I said to Shippy, "Let's stop and have tea in the beautiful lounge. There's plenty of time."

"No," he said adamantly. "We'll get something at the airport." Grumbling inside and disappointed, I nevertheless acquiesced, and off we went to the airport.

There we found seats not far from the counter where soft drinks were served. "We can go over and get a drink there," Shippy suggested. I picked up my large tote bag to move to the counter, but Shippy put his coat over his bag and started to leave.

"You are not going to leave your bag there, are you?" I questioned, aghast at the thought.

"We're only going over there," he pointed. "I'll keep my eye on it."

I continued to protest. "Don't leave your bag there. It's not safe." I had no success. "Well," I said, with an edge to my voice. "I'm not leaving mine," and off we went.

You can guess the rest of the story. When we returned, his bag was gone. What you probably couldn't guess is the magnitude of the loss. In that case were all of Shippy's notes on his work thus far on the trip, his expensive camera and all the pictures we had taken, his immunization papers and officials documents, as well as our tickets and schedule for the rest of the trip! Our suitcases were already on our flight to Manila, as we were near boarding time. There I stood, clutching my tote bag that held emergency items in case my suitcase was lost.

For the first time in my life (and the last, I might add), I saw my strong husband, always in command of himself and circumstances, totally devastated. There was no way I could say, "I told you so." We both needed all the help we could give each other. We notified police at the airport, but there was little they could do. We had no choice but to stay in Hong Kong and try to regroup.

We tried first to get a room again at the Peninsula, but it was full. Across the street there was another hotel, fortunately, with an available room. The only thing I remember about that hotel was a door with long, colored, jingling beads swaying back and forth like I had seen in old Chinese movies. We dropped off my bag and headed directly for the United States Embassy. Thank God for the Embassy! They started the process to replace Shippy's passport and gave us both all our shots again since the inoculation records were also lost. Even more difficult, Shippy had to reconstruct the rest of his trip and try to recreate the notes on his work that he had made so far. I then went into nearby shops to buy a few necessary items to keep Shippy looking presentable. I had my tote bag, but he had *nothing*. Our bags, hopefully, were waiting for us in Manila.

With the excellent help of the American Embassy, we were winging our way to Manila three days later. Fortunately, our luggage was awaiting us there, safe and sound. My last words to my husband as we laid our crisis to rest were, "Now will you listen to me when I tell you something in the future?"

"Oh yes," he replied. "You are an angel! I will always listen to you!" (What do *you* think? Did he or didn't he?)

The second experience from our Bank trips that I want to mention relates to my positive view of safety in air travel. We were flying on JAL (Japanese Airlines) from Tokyo to Manila on the last leg of our second World Bank trip. About halfway to our destination, I noticed some flames coming out of one of the engines. The captain, an American on contract to JAL, informed us that we had a serious engine problem and he had decided to return to Tokyo. On arrival back at Tokyo, we jettisoned fuel and landed safely. Actually, I don't recall any great sense of uneasiness over the emergency, but of course, all of us on board were happy to set foot on Japan's solid ground. In a replacement aircraft, we finally arrived in Manila, albeit somewhat late, where we had a pleasant visit in a fascinating city. I write this because in all my miles of air travel, this was the only serious crisis or airplane malfunction I experienced.

This episode was not without its positive aspects. While waiting in the airport for a replacement aircraft, I browsed through all the jewelry in the shops and bought a pair of unique earrings. I wear them often and am invariably asked about them. Thus my airplane story is told again, and the episode remains fresh in my memory.

One of the rewarding features (among many, I might add) of our World Bank years was the number of interesting people we met from around the world. I was always thrilled to see the flags of many nations flying in the breeze outside the main entrance to the Bank Building in downtown Washington, D.C., representing the diversity of Bank personnel. There was much entertaining and social life, which we enjoyed, and we never tired of showing our visitors from abroad the historic sights and beauty of Washington. I also took full advantage of all the museums and activities offered in D.C. With the Kennedy Center, my cup overflowed with the opportunities it offered in every area of the arts. I never missed a ballet! It was a full and busy time, but Gwen, Marie, and I kept the Monday morning prayer time together sacrosanct. We were growing in the Lord and in friendship with our inner-city friends.

Unfortunately, this happy time was clouded by concerns for my mother. My father had died while I was in Egypt, and my mother had been living by herself. She had reached an age where it was difficult to continue living alone. My brother, with his family of six children, was unable to have her live with him. I flew to Minnesota to look over a nursing home they were considering. I found I could not leave her there, so we decided to bring her to Washington. To accommodate her, we added a room onto the house, complete with private bathroom. It wasn't until I reached an age where I felt it necessary to leave my house for other living arrangements that I understood how difficult it must have been for her to leave family and friends in Minnesota. However, she was a dear, sweet, wonderful woman, and we had happy times together. Bruce was especially caring of Mother, even though he lived in Connecticut at the time, having been ordained an Episcopalian priest after studying at General Seminary in New York. During the six years she was with us, he offered to have her stay with him so I could take a trip to Europe with Shippy. He also spent time with her on other occasions and provided many thoughtful gifts.

After six years with us, Mother died after a short illness. We returned to her longtime home in Minneapolis for the funeral. My brother's four sons along with Bruce and Richard were the pallbearers. Two of the greatest gifts given to me were a mother who set an example that influenced my life profoundly for good, and a father who cared for me, shared his love of history with me, and in general, had a sense of humor and joie de vivre that I enjoyed.

18

Revelation and Forgiveness

A few months after returning to Washington from my mother's funeral, I was working around the house, my thoughts on mundane matters, when suddenly it seemed as if a light illuminated the deepest part of my being. All at once I saw myself as I was, selfish and proud. There were no "signs or wonders," and I had no unusual emotional reactions except a deep conviction of sin and acceptance that this was indeed true. Moreover, my selfishness was revealed to me in the context of my beloved mother. I saw that I had cared for her more out of a sense of duty than with a heart overflowing with love, which she so richly deserved. I understood for the first time what Ezekiel meant in 11:19 when he wrote, "then I will give them one heart and I will put a new spirit within them, and take the stony heart out of their flesh and give them a heart of flesh" (KJV).

I fell to my knees, as I had done so many times before in my deep need, and asked forgiveness. I prayed for the heart of unselfish love that I so much needed. Only a new life within me with a new heart was my salvation. Jesus then did for me what I could not do for myself. He gave me His very life to live my life for me, and He gave me His great loving heart to be my heart from now on until He takes me with Him into eternal life. In my spiritual Quest,

I was now brought to the point where I received Jesus as my *Savior,* and my *life as His new life was born in me.*

From that moment on, I was broken and humbled. I would never look upon anyone sinning without thinking, "There but for the grace of God, go I." I never forgot that the sins of selfishness and pride were among those most strongly condemned by Jesus. As with every experience we share with our Lord, there was a positive outcome. It was now safe for the Lord to use me more freely. I learned humility and compassion and was, as the Bible says, "a new creature in Christ" (2 Cor. 5:17). To Him be all the glory.

However, there was a period of time that followed when I had difficulty forgiving myself pertaining to my mother. It wasn't what I did, but what I didn't do that troubled me. At that time, I did not have enough unselfish love in my heart. However, Mother's unconditional love never changed. I learned that unselfish love is not easy to attain. It is only easy when it does not cost you at your levels of deepest pleasures and desires. Caring for mother cost me the opportunity to travel with my husband on all his South American trips. I "kicked against the pricks." I realized I was thinking more of myself than her needs. How difficult it must have been for her to leave her home and friends and the family in Minnesota. I could have given her more time and more love. However, she, in her pure spirit, always looked upon me as a perfect daughter, which only made me feel worse!

There was no question in my mind about my mother's forgiveness nor Jesus' forgiveness, but I still could not forgive myself. In time, however, I came to see that this state of mind was a lack of faith on my part, as Jesus promised that if we confess our sins, He is faithful to forgive our sins and cleanse us from all unrighteousness (1 John 1:9). However, the forgiveness of self was still not easy. I found help in my devotional book *God Calling*. Jesus is speaking:

Often I have to shield my disciples from their own scorn. My poor Peter could never have done My work, never have had the courage to live on, or the daring to live for Me (after he had denied me three times), but for the tender love with which I enwrapped him.

I also, like Peter, "enwrapped" in Jesus' love, was able to accept His forgiveness and go forward humbly to serve him.

I have learned to take very seriously the words in the Lord's Prayer, "Forgive us our trespasses as we forgive those who trespass against us." I have had cause in my lifetime for unforgiveness toward others, but my own need for it has given me, along with God's grace, the gift of forgiveness. I was brought to the fullness of Jesus' salvation through the grace of God and the unconditional love and forgiveness of my mother. It is a sobering thought that I will be forgiven only as I forgive others. That is God's word in the Lord's Prayer. With His grace enabling me, I dare not disobey Him.

19

The Cambodian Refugees

Shippy was Chairman of the Commission on Missions at our nearby church. I was also a member, as we were both interested in the work of the mission field around the world. Unrest was rampant in Vietnam and Cambodia as North Vietnam became an increasing threat to their territorial integrity, and refugees were fleeing in great numbers to safety. The churches were sponsoring many of these refugees, and our commission recommended that we accept one of these families through the channels of our church headquarters. It was necessary to gain the acceptance of this project by the whole church, and our commission set to work. We learned all the information that we could through the church itself and other channels and then shared it with the entire congregation. The vote "yea or nay" had to go through designated channels of church order in each congregation requesting a refugee family.

We had two strong leaders on our Commission of Missions. One was my husband, and the other was a man of extensive experience in the foreign service field, where he left an imprint of impressive accomplishment. Above all, he had a warm, caring heart. The rest of the commission members were equally dedicated men and women, and with little negative response by the church as a whole, the project was approved. We waited with anticipation for the news that a family was to be ours.

At last, the call came that our family had been chosen! They were from Cambodia, a young medical doctor and his wife with three children, two boys and a baby, also a boy. We started our preparations in earnest now, as they would be arriving December 10.

Predictably, our first efforts were to find a place for them to live. After days of searching, we found a house in the area that was suitable but needed a good deal of "tender, loving care." The members of the commission and any others interested rolled up their sleeves and went to work to clean up the house and purchase the necessities of life for them. Among all of us there was a spirit of joy and fellowship in our shared experience that radiated among us. One group of ladies did nothing but find clothes and articles for the needs of the baby. The rummage sale, held every year, was a source of treasure for this particular group. They enthusiastically gleaned all the best baby accessories and basic needs they could find there!

A friend and I delegated ourselves to the bathroom, which was in great need of help. My friend was and is a lovely lady, and around that time her husband was head of one the major agencies in Washington, D.C. We went to work on our hands and knees in this grungy, grimy bathroom, scrubbing away merrily. There were other "scrubbers" also, as there was much to do in this house, especially the bathroom!

At long last December 10 arrived, and Terry, Ray, Shippy, and I (the two chairmen and their wives) started for National Airport (as it was called at that time). The new immigrants stepped off the airplane, and we walked toward them and they toward us, the young mother carrying the baby and the father with two small boys by the hand. We were all overcome with emotion.

Somehow we put them all into one car and drove off to the house in Maryland, where a fire had been started in the fireplace and church members were waiting to greet the new arrivals. The warmth and glow of the open fireplace was our master stroke! Food was brought in after escorting them around their new home. On entering the baby's room and seeing all the baby clothes arranged so carefully and lovingly, the weary mother looked into our eyes and said tearfully, "How can we ever thank you?"

So began a long and happy relationship with Dr. Pemy Chhim, his lovely wife Thari, and their three sons. Love flowed freely between them and the entire congregation. Their English improved rapidly, and the commission and the congregation decided to extend our support to them for two years instead of the usual more limited time. This decision was made so that Pemy would not have to sacrifice his career as a medical doctor and could continue to practice in the United States. This he accomplished.

There is so much more to tell but it is not possible in this book. In time, they moved to Baltimore, and it was more difficult to keep in close touch with them. However, we did see them over a long period of time. They all came to visit us as well as our visiting them. When Shippy was ill, they were faithful to come to Bethesda to visit him in the hospital. At his death, they were present at his Memorial Service.

I love Thari and the Chhim family. Many times in my later years, I wished they still lived in the old house near O'Donnell's Restaurant and I could stop by and chat with Thari and we could have lunch together. I remember her pain when I took her to the dentist to have extensive work done on her teeth. It was a traumatic experience, but she endured it bravely. I suffered with her.

I treasure the photograph she sent me the Christmas before last of herself and her husband. They looked so well and happy. They are a precious part of the mosaic of my life.

20

Day by Day in Washington

My life continued, interesting and stimulating, in Washington. The days passed swiftly in a variety of experiences, both mundane and otherwise.

One of the "otherwise" experiences was a reception, given by President Macapagal of the Philippines when he was on a State visit to Washington, in honor of President Lyndon Johnson. I must confess, I was hoping we might be invited to the White House for the welcoming dinner traditionally given for visiting heads of state. Shippy had met the Philippine President while conferring with him on a World Bank project in Manila. Alas, my hopes were dashed. We were not invited.

However, we were delighted to be invited by President Macapagal to a return reception for President Johnson. It was a lavish affair, and I enjoyed myself immensely. I shook hands with President Johnson, and we had a brief chat on non-essential matters. His personality was forceful, and I remember his eyes were penetrating and focused. They seemed to be focused on my outer- rather than my inner-self as he commented that he liked my dress. I was amused, because I remembered reading that the president often chose clothes for Lady Bird and their daughters. Lucy, the younger daughter, had accompanied him to the reception, and I wondered to myself if he had chosen her lovely dress. I also wondered to myself as I was writing this why I didn't keep that dress. I gave it away when I moved from Washington in later years, and it still fit me perfectly.

A second "otherwise" experience was the World Bank Christmas party. After going through the receiving line and greeting Robert McNamara, who was then president of the World Bank, we stepped into the huge ballroom of one of the leading Washington hotels. There we saw a vision that even a Hollywood spectacle would find hard to equal. Two orchestras were playing, one in the main room and another in an adjoining room. Serving tables displayed lavish platters of food representing all manner of cuisine and ethnic origin. Having a sweet tooth that is only partially controlled, I hovered over the dessert table. At first, each table was so beautiful that I could not bear to disturb any of them. I felt it was sacrilegious to touch anything displayed with such artistry. It was as if Renoir or Monet had been busy overseeing their underlings in the kitchen! In a short time, however, I overcame my hesitancy.

I thought back to the captain's dinner on the *Gripsholm*, thinking nothing could surpass that. This did, in size, if nothing else. However, that was to be the last of the large World Bank Christmas parties. Following that party, there were criticisms from various sources about the expense involved in this celebration. The World Bank responded promptly, and from then on small interdepartmental celebrations became the norm. I agreed with this decision and commend the Bank for acting immediately and decisively. In my inner-city work, I could understand the gulf between the two worlds. The money could be put to better use.

However, a lingering nostalgia remained. As with the captain's dinner on the *Gripsholm* and our return from overseas, it seemed I was always saying farewell to some era of my life, albeit for better or for worse. I guess this is life, and one must let go of one part and step forward into another. However, the memories still float around me like gauzy streamers encircling me, never letting me be free.

A third "otherwise" experience related to Abraham Lincoln and Washington, D.C. Abraham Lincoln is my favorite president, and there are many books about his life on my shelves. The Ford Theater in downtown Washington, where Lincoln was shot, was one of my favorite places to share with visitors. Also, the Anderson House, where the President was taken after he was shot and where he died, is sacrosanct to me. The entire tragedy becomes reality before your eyes as you see the bed in which he died after viewing the box in the theater where he was shot. I also found inspiration in visiting the Lincoln Memorial and reading his unforgettable words inscribed therein.

A final "otherwise" experience in Washington was the annual Fourth of July celebration. It was a wonderful time to be in Washington, D.C. Our grandchildren were often with us, and we had our own special place at the Mall to celebrate. Laden with food, drink, chairs, blankets, and Frisbees, we arrived early and settled in for a joyous day of celebration culminating in what must be one of the greatest fireworks displays in the country.

The most exciting Fourth was July 4, 1976, celebrating the U.S. bicentennial. We arrived at noon at a green, grassy spot near the Washington Monument and staked our claim. The spirit of everyone was euphoric. We rejoiced, one and all, in celebrating this historic day in our country's history. The fireworks reached a new level of spectacular beauty and excitement as burst after burst of fiery color set the sky aflame.

It was long after midnight when we finally reached home. The crowds were huge and the traffic congested as we crawled along the streets inch by inch. But nothing dimmed the enthusiasm of the people. Everyone was singing and waving flags and really not wanting to leave. What a privilege it had been to be a part of this historic day. God bless America!

It was a gift in my life to be set down in Washington, D.C. The winds that started in World War II, blowing me from place to place like that leaf in a storm, had blessed me by allowing me to stay for thirty years in one place before lifting me again into a different world.

21

Memories around the World

As the years in Washington went by, my days of international travel were drawing to a close. I had so many memories from these trips that "filled my heart with pleasure" that I must share some thoughts along this line as they come to mind.

I quote from William Wordsworth's poem again:

> For oft when on my couch I lie
> In vacant or in pensive mood
> They flash upon that inward eye
> Which is the bliss of solitude,
> And then my heart with pleasure fills
> And dances with the daffodils.

And indeed my heart "did fill with pleasure and danced with the daffodils" those many years ago with Bruce in the English lake country on his spring break from Oxford University. However, in later years, on my two world trips, I added other memories that I will share as they come to mind.

Evensong at York Minster, England. Old walls clustered around the great Cathedral, with the daffodils covering them like a blanket of gold. Glorious, colorful beauty shining through the stained glass windows. The quiet to meditate on the majesty of God. The special joy to be there with my son.

The Nile River, Egypt: Watching the feluccas drifting along the river past us while relaxing at our modest yacht club. They seemed to glide effortlessly along the tree-lined banks, their white sails propelling them as if touched by a magic wand and changed into wings. Lazily, we watched them one by one drift out of sight.

Bangkok, Thailand: Traveling by boat along the *klongs* in Bangkok, the waterways bursting with life along the way. Merchants approaching in all manner of water-borne conveyance. Houses along the shore, shops lining each side—a water-borne life and community, exciting and fascinating.

El Alamein, Egypt: Vast expanses of desert with imprints of war still visible in the hot sand. Rows and rows of crosses in the graveyards—Italian, German, American. We picked up a German helmet left behind by one mother's son—the devastating cost of war. I wept.

Agra, India: The Taj Mahal at dawn reflecting the soft sky as the sun was awakening into life. The beauty of this exquisite temple dedicated to love that has enchanted the world—I find no words to express its glory. It far surpassed our expectations. We left its presence, forever enriched. "A thing of beauty is a joy forever. Its loveliness increases, it will never pass into nothingness" (John Keats).

Cairo, Egypt: Observing the stars on a night in the desert—no lavish display of diamonds has ever sparkled brighter than the stars in the heavens looking down on the Pyramids. The desert itself—its vastness, serenity, and its power seep into your soul; you feel at one with eternity.

Taipai, Taiwan: Being chauffeured back to the Grand Hotel after Shippy misunderstood that the dinner we were going to was a "men's only" affair. *Grand* was a perfect name for this hotel. The lobby itself would render speechless the most jaded traveler. I chose the Chinese dining room that evening for my favorite food and ate by myself. I managed the chopsticks tentatively but finished my plate with relish.

Kyoto, Japan: Eating breakfast and gazing out the window at a distant temple hiding among the trees with a glimmer of gold peeking out from time to time, from origins I could not distinguish. The temple seemed to float in the morning mist. Kyoto—a gem of delicate beauty.

Seoul, Korea: An opportunity to see and share with Shippy a country where he spent the year during the Korean War. A pleasure to meet John Underwood, of the Underwood family of Presbyterian missionaries, who Shippy met during his year there. Gracious hospitality given to us. Sightseeing with those especially knowledgeable about the country.

Lahore, Pakistan: Being wakened by a knock on my hotel door by a young Pakistani girl sent to take me sightseeing—a charming companion. Walking and walking and purchasing a lovely native doll that resembled my companion. A visit to the American School in Lahore—I wonder if it is still there. I enjoyed a gracious and interesting visit, too short a stay to see as much as I wished of the Pakistani people.

And so many more! My memory storehouse is filled to overflowing. As I grow older, it is a privilege and joy to have this well stocked treasure chest to reach into in leisure moments. This I do not do at the expense of my present life, however, which is rewarding in itself, day by day. I have named the condo where I now live my "Halfway House to Heaven." It is indeed just that.

22

Family

My Quest for spiritual growth would not be complete without mentioning the people most important in my life: my family. Therefore, if you will allow me a brief digression, I would like to share a little about my family.

From the time I was a small child, I disliked my name. To have the surname of Brown was bad enough, but for my parents to put the two-syllable name of *Lois* before it was the final blow. Why couldn't I have had a name like Gardener (visions of flowers) or Farnsworth (visions of dignity and respect) or Jefferson (visions of the President)?

I toyed with the names of Juliana Jefferson or Felicia Farnsworth. But there I was—plain Lois Brown! The *Helen* in between (after my grandmother) didn't help one bit. I lived with this dilemma until my marriage to Harold Shipman, at age 23, and at once "deep-sixed" the *Brown*.

Now, in the twilight of my years, I have come to a change in heart. I had one brother, who was a gifted musician, and he and his wife had seven children, one lost tragically as an infant. There are four nephews and two nieces in my family today. It was difficult to be in close touch with all of them while living abroad for many years. Letters do not make up for direct contact. When I returned to the United States and settled in the Washington, D.C., area, I made an effort to restore contact with my family. Each year I returned to Minnesota for a visit in order to know them all more closely.

Fortunately, one nephew moved to a Virginia suburb of Washington, D.C., and I was able to draw closer to him and his family. Another nephew visited us in Chevy Chase along with my brother and sister-in-law. The youngest nephew also visited us, and we became close to him.

I found my nieces and nephews to be fun-loving and good company, as we all shared an Irish heritage from my father and paternal grandmother, Mary Delaney, who was straight out of Ireland. They are all articulate, with a serious side—yet leavened by humor and a vital sense of living. My brother died recently, but my sister-in-law in Minneapolis still has a special place in my heart.

I knew innately the importance of family. We need to be part of a group that cares and takes responsibility for each other. The family unit has been the core of civilization for ages.

As I mellowed in my later years, so did I mellow regarding my name. I have reclaimed the name of Brown and now use my full name, Lois Brown Shipman. I feel content. I am one of the Brown family. I belong.

I belong also to the Shipman family. Richard's children, Kristina and David, are super-special to me in a way that only grandmothers understand. Shippy's relatives are my relatives also, and I am in touch with them. As for my Bruce and Richard, I consider them perfect—well, almost! My joy is complete when I am with them. My cup runneth over. "Felicia Farnsworth" is longed for no more.

It was this love of family and the desire to reunite regularly that led Shippy and me to purchase two weeks of time-sharing at a house on Shipyard Plantation in Hilton Head, South Carolina. We wanted it to be a place where our family could gather together and relax, and we could keep in touch with one another. For almost seventeen years now, various members of the family have met regularly at this paradise in the "low country" of South Carolina. It has been one of the happiest experiences of my life.

Somewhere in my primeval past, I must have been a Southerner. Stepping off that airplane so many years ago during World War II into the December sunshine and warmth of Mobile, Alabama, I felt I was coming home. I melded into the ambiance around me like a native who had been away for years and finally had found her way back after being lost in the snow of Minnesota.

I do not wish to say one word against that wonderful world of ice and snow and tobogganing and skating and all manner of winter sports and thirty-degrees-below-zero weather. It was beautiful and awe-inspiring, but somehow I couldn't quite enter into it all wholeheartedly. My skating was less than mediocre, and tobogganing always found me clambering out of mounds of snow feeling very cold.

Somehow, I think that Minnesota, with all its wonders, was made for someone hardier than myself. It seemed to demand of me more than I had within me to give. I never condemned beautiful, wonderful Minnesota. It was I who never seemed to measure up to its expectations. It had so much to offer me but I seemed to short-change it in reciprocation. It had all that weather to test my sense of exhilaration and endurance, and winter sports of unbelievable fun and excitement, but I always seemed to fall short in experiencing these satisfying emotions. I truly loved Minnesota, but I felt she was sorely disappointed in this native daughter she had produced.

When I discovered the South, I found few challenges. Even the flying cockroaches I learned to respect, if not exactly admire! But when I found Mobile and later Hilton Head Island, I sank into a revelry of delight! I could sit for hours just dreaming and looking at the flowers in full bloom around me. Resting in the afternoon in Hilton Head, I would gaze out my window at a moss-hung oak tree. These great trees, with their garlands of moss, always gave me a touch of delirium. The marshlands evoked only a little less adoration, and if a white Ibis appeared in their midst, it was almost more joy than I could contain. The camellias, with their waxy purity, were too perfect to be real and sent me into spasms of delight.

As I return to Hilton Head each May, the transformation begins. I am like a benevolent Jekyl and Hyde. My heart skips a beat as I see my first moss-hung oak tree again, and I feel the change coming upon me. I become a Southern Lady in body, mind, and spirit, lacking only the hoop skirt! I am transported into the new ambiance around me and filled to overflowing with joy and contentment.

When it is time to return to my other more sedate life, I go willingly. I am transformed back into my more brisk, orderly self. However, the happy thought stays deep in my mind that my carpet bag is packed and ready for my next trip south in May.

There are several other people who must be mentioned when talking about family. They are Hans, my Grandfather and Grandmother Pierce, and my cousin Helen.

Hans. I look upon Hans as my third son. He lives next door to me, has been a caretaker and companion, and has enabled me to live independently after I sold my house in Maryland.

Hans and Bruce met many years ago while Bruce was studying to become an Episcopalian priest at General Seminary in New York. He was born in Germany and raised in the midst of the suffering and desolation of World War II. His father had been held as a prisoner of war in Russia and returned home very near death.

In his late teens, Hans immigrated to the United States, where one sister was married and lived in the Midwest. There, in the heartland of our country, he began life in a strange town whose people spoke a different language. He struggled for mastery of English, having no previous education in the language.

Hans found work at Madison General Hospital in Madison, Wisconsin, and spent four years training in surgery and assisting in various operations. His skill in surgical procedures became so evident that one of the chief surgeons at the hospital offered to finance his education in this field. Primarily because of his difficulty with English, he decided to become a specialist in the use of the electron microscope. He was subsequently recruited by Yale University where he worked for seventeen years in the cell biology department under the guidance of George Palade, who was awarded the Nobel Prize in 1974 in this field.

Hans is now a scientist at Pfizer, Inc., doing similar work—evaluating the positive or negative effects of certain drugs on human beings. He has been part of our family for many years—and he is an excellent cook!

Grandfather and Grandmother Pierce. I never knew my maternal Grandfather Pierce; he died before I was born. However, he played an important role in my life, albeit an unusual one. Named after the "father of our country," he bore the name George Washington Pierce with pride. He served in the Civil War in Company "C" of the Eleventh Maine Regiment. He was injured during the war, returned to civilian life, and died at a comparatively young age. His widow, my Grandmother Pierce, came to live with us at this time. She was a staunch patriot and a proud charter member in the Minnesota chapter of the Women's Relief Corps of the GAR (Grand Army of the Republic).

The Quest

A love for my country was born and nourished over the years in the roots of my childhood. I was raised on Memorial Day ceremonies honoring veterans over the years and memorized patriotic poems such as "In Flander's Fields the Poppies Grow" and others in memory of men who had given their lives for our country. Lincoln's Gettysburg Address was a must, and I could recite it word for word at any time or any place.

Grandmother Pierce had a small Civil War widow's pension from the government, earned by my grandfather's service and his injury. I was graduating from high school in the midst of the Great Depression of the early '30s. I longed for a college education, but there was no way my parents could afford the tuition, even though we lived close enough to the University of Minnesota that I could live at home. I determined to earn some money using the typing skills I had learned in high school, but this was nowhere near enough to finance a full course load in order to graduate in four years. At this point, my grandmother offered me part of her widow's pension, the only independent means she had. It was enough to enable me to graduate in four years from the College of Education with a B.S. degree (given at that time, but not now), aided by odd jobs along the way.

I was able to express my love and appreciation in person to my grandmother, but as I look back, not with the depth of gratitude and love that I feel today. Youth takes too much for granted, especially from its family.

The only picture I have of my grandfather is hanging on my bedroom wall. As I look at it, I have three wishes: I wish I could have known him. I wish I could have told him that he was a big part of the college diploma that I proudly held in my hand so long ago. Most of all, I wish I could have told him "I love you, Grandfather, and I am proud of you. Your granddaughter will never forget you."

My Cousin Helen: One of the unexpected joys of Washington, D.C., was meeting for the first time my long-lost cousin, Helen. Our mothers were first cousins and had been born and raised in Minneapolis, Minnesota. After marriage, Helen's mother, Elizabeth, left Minnesota, and Helen was raised elsewhere. I had heard about her all my life, as photographs and correspondence passed between our mothers. On arriving in Washington, my mother wrote me that Helen and her family lived in the area and for me to call her. Helen's mother did likewise, informing her that I lived nearby. Neither of us did anything about it.

On one of my mother's visits from Minneapolis after we arrived in Washington, her first question was, "Have you called Helen yet?"

"No," I said apologetically.

Straight to the telephone directory she went, and Helen was invited at once for a visit As Helen was walking up the steps, Mother looked out the window and exclaimed, "She looks just like Elizabeth!" (her much-loved cousin).

Thus began my friendship with my second cousin, Helen, and her dear daughter, Mary, that has blessed all of our lives. It was an especially cherished relationship for me, as I had been raised with one brother, two male cousins, and no girls near my own age. I yearned for the companionship and warmth of a girl cousin. Helen fit into that role perfectly. She was younger (but not by too many years), pretty, and we were compatible at once. Together we shared a sense of humor and had many laughs, as well as serious times.

The serious times deepened on Helen's return from California. She had left Washington with her family when her husband was transferred to a new location on the West Coast. On her return to the Washington area, I found she was experiencing a period of great stress. During her absence I had also encountered difficult circumstances, which had led me in search of strength and inner peace to meet them. During that search, a friend had invited me to attend an ecumenical group of women who met for Bible study in one member's home. The group was led by an exceptional teacher, and it was there that I found much needed spiritual food. I learned what it meant to be "born again" and receive Jesus' new life within me. The teaching of John 3:3 became real to me when I read Jesus' reply to Nicodemus, "Jesus answered and said to him, 'Most assuredly I say to you, unless one is born again he cannot see the Kingdom of God'" (KJV).

Jesus said to him, "I am the Way, the Truth, and the Life. No one comes to the Father except through me" (John 14:6). It is *his* life that must be born within us, and we receive that new life by faith. Thus I received Jesus' life and reaffirmed my willingness to learn and grow in Him.

I shared my experiences and my own need with Helen and gave her a copy of a devotional book I cherished. I then introduced her to my Bible study group, and there we both found spiritual nourishment and growth within this dedicated group of women, led by a gifted and inspiring teacher. Helen gave her life to Jesus and is now an integral part of that group, which still meets today.

Due to our various needs, spiritual and otherwise, we set up what we named our "Nine o'clock Hot Line" to call for help and sharing through the years. Due to the many times of family and personal crises we endured together, we named ourselves "Scarlett" and "Melanie," after the two characters in *Gone with the Wind* who were beset with family crises.

Every summer we had a membership in a swimming pool in nearby Bethesda. Helen, who did not live far from me, her daughter Mary, and I swam, ate, talked about Jesus, laughed, discussed anything and everything, and enjoyed ourselves immensely!

One of our many shared crisis experiences was with my aging mother. In later years, I brought my mother from Minneapolis to live with us. In her ninetieth year, I took her to Minneapolis for a last visit. While there she contacted a cold that weakened her, but she was still able to fly and I was anxious to get her home safely. However, we did not realize the extent of her weakness. Shippy was away, and upon arriving in Washington, I needed help. I called Helen and said, "This is Scarlett. I need you. Shippy is away and Mother is not well. I can't manage her alone in D.C."

Her reply was, "Okay, dear, Melanie is at your service. Give me the flight time and I'll be there. See you!"

On arrival, aided by the flight crew, Mother was extricated from her seat and put into a wheelchair, and we were on our way to Helen's car. With help, Mother was finally ensconced in the back seat, and we were off to Chevy Chase and home.

Unfortunately, our house was located on a raised terrace with many steps. We decided to take Mother in the garage entrance, which had stairs in the basement and a railing leading to the first floor. Dear Mother! By the time she was out of the car, supported by Helen and me, she stopped at the foot of the stairs and could go no further. How could we get her up the flight of stairs to safe ground? *What to do? What to do?*

Helen was a former airline stewardess (you can guess by the name, the era of her employment!), and the first thing she said was, "We must take off her glasses!" Off came the glasses. Neither Helen nor I are especially robust, but we each took an arm, a deep breath, and heaved upward. We had absolutely no success. Mother was a total dead weight! *What to do? What to do?*

I finally said, "I'd better call a neighbor for help." Helen agreed, so off we went across the street, returning with Mr. L. With the three of us exerting maximum effort, we finally managed to get her to safe ground.

At long last she was safely in bed. With a smile she reached for the little pillow with which she slept. Helen and I looked at each other, and between laughs and tears, we tucked her in.

This was only one of our shared exploits. We now call each other "Scarmel," short for both famous names! Alas, we are now separated by the miles between us, but our spirits still vibrate together on the telephone, even though our exploits are now but memories.

Part Four:
The End of the Quest

23

I Find Myself a Widow

The easy flow of the days in Washington was abruptly interrupted when Shippy experienced a heart attack. His hospital stay was short, however, and he was soon working again. Shippy had retired from the World Bank after fifteen years' service but continued to work as a consultant both for the Bank and other companies.

Our fiftieth wedding anniversary was approaching about this time, and we were planning to have a large party in Minneapolis at the Women's Club. Unfortunately, this much anticipated event had to be canceled when Shippy had another heart attack. This one was more serious than the first and culminated in a five-artery bypass operation. After an extended recovery, which was prolonged by a serious infection, Shippy was able to return to work again.

We enjoyed together a conference in San Juan, Puerto Rico, and another in Panama, where I especially enjoyed seeing the Panama Canal and watching a large ship pass through the locks. Some time later, he and two other engineers flew to Taipei, Taiwan, to work on a water problem there. It was his last project. An infection sent him into the hospital again, and a serious operation followed. He lived only a few more months and died on April 8, 1992.

We had a simple memorial service at our church in Chevy Chase, surrounded by loving friends, family, and

Shippy's coworkers. Thari and Pemy, our Cambodian friends, drove from Baltimore to be with us. All three of our inner-city families attended the service.

In times past, I had found Jesus to be my *friend*, my *teacher*, and my *master*. Now, at the time of my husband's sickness and death, I found Jesus during those difficult years as my *comforter*. During this time, the pain was deep and the need profound. I was not carried through on velvet-covered cushions, but underneath me were the everlasting arms of love, of someone who knew the meaning of pain. There I found a closer union with Jesus as I shared my Garden of Gethesmane with Him.

Tributes to Shippy's life continued well beyond the funeral. One particularly meaningful memorial appeared in the magazine of AIDIS, the Association of Inter-American Sanitary Engineers. Shippy was an active supporter of AIDIS, a *Miembro Distinguido* (distinguished member), and a former president of the USA section. The article paid tribute to his career, highlighting his accomplishments at PAHO and the World Bank. At PAHO, he was cited for his work that led to "greater emphasis on water supply" in Latin America. At the World Bank, the article noted, "He was the leader in the water supply and sanitation program for the Bank, and established the standard of behavior and performance for the rest of the engineers and the financial analysts working on water supply projects." The article concluded with a summary of Shippy's professional awards and citations. He was a Fellow of the American Society of Civil Engineers and the American Public Health Association, a member of the National Society of Professional Engineers, a Diplomat of the American Academy of Environmental Engineers, and was Chairman of the 1971 United Nations Interagency Subcommittee on Water Resources. He received citations from the governments of Korea, Israel, Egypt, and Bolivia and was awarded the Friendship Medal by the British Institute of Water Engineers. He was also a Centennial Fellow of the Johns Hopkins University. The article was especially meaningful to me because it was written by and for the people he worked with, including many of our personal friends.

Shortly after Shippy's memorial service, Julie and her husband Gerald picked me up at my house on a sparkling spring day that revealed Chevy Chase and Washington, D.C., in all its beauty. The flowers were bursting into bloom and the cherry trees around the tidal basin were luring many admirers, including ourselves, to marvel at their loveliness. Julie and Gerald were taking me to lunch at the Cosmos Club, which had excellent food plus a charming decor and ambiance that always lifted my spirits. That evening, tired in mind and body, I realized I was now assuming a new role in life. I found myself a widow.

Our afternoon together helped to start the healing process after Shippy's death. The new life springing up from months of earthy darkness and now reflecting beauty and joyful life affected me as a good tonic and also a lesson in life. I had been in a dark period of my life, but now Shippy was at rest. I realized that I had to try to reemerge, just as the flowers and trees around me were emerging into something worthwhile. What did I have to give to others?

Pondering this thought, I reflected on my talents and remembered I had been a teacher in Egypt. Chevy Chase Elementary School was not far from my house, so I decided to volunteer in any area where they might be able to use me.

I loved returning to a school environment. I was given work primarily with foreign-born students who needed extra help with the curriculum. I felt happy and fulfilled as I received my volunteer certificate at the end of the school year.

Unexpectedly, another opportunity opened up for me, together with Gwen and Marie. Changes had occurred in our lives as the years passed, and although we were still meeting together, our work in the inner city had almost ceased. Marie and I were driving to an outlying area around Washington to have lunch together. This was really an unheard of experience for us, as Gwen, Marie, and I never did socialize together. We were too busy going in and out of the inner city or celebrating holidays with our families, to say nothing of our lives at home.

However, Marie's responsibilities had decreased with the death of a mother-in-law, and Shippy had died, so we were freer than we had been for some time. During our lunch together, we were reminiscing about some of our times in the past when we had hosted gatherings for young women at Gwen's lovely home in Potomac. We would invite Christian speakers who we knew were especially gifted in sharing their faith with others. All of a sudden, the thought came to both of us, Why couldn't we do something like that again? We contacted Gwen and started to plan, of course, always under the Lord's guidance. So began "The Teacuppers," one of our most cherished endeavors.

I had a large empty house, so we began meeting there. We decided to have a tea and invite any women in nearby churches who wished to come. Marie had a daughter-in-law in the "young married" group in a church nearby, so we started there. For our first "tea party" we invited an outstanding Christian lady, who was in demand as a speaker and fortunately was able to give us a day. I unearthed all the teacups I had collected and took out the best of my linens and silver. The day arrived, and it was a big success!

Gwen, Marie, and I then discussed where to go from there. We decided to have one more tea and then ask the girls what they would prefer: teas and speakers every other week or a Bible study on the same time schedule. The girls responded with "the Bible study." We were off and running!

From then on, we met at my home with approximately –fifteen to twenty young mothers. Marie did the major task of teaching, although I assisted and taught during the summer. Gwen assumed the financial responsibility for the babysitting. Later, the girls themselves handled this. They named themselves the "Teacuppers," and so they remain to this day.

After Shippy's death, I joined Fourth Presbyterian Church in Bethesda, Maryland. As a child of twelve years, I was baptized at the same time as my mother at Andrew Presbyterian Church in southeast Minneapolis and brought up in the church there. The baptism at her side is still vivid in my memory. Somehow I felt I did not want to break that bond with her. Her positive influence on my life has been profound. She took me by the hand to church and her life reflected the truth she found there.

This is no way diminishes my love and appreciation for my many years at Chevy Chase Methodist Church. It was there where I met Gwen and Marie, and it was there that I found a church family and was nourished in the Christian faith and the love of Jesus. Those years in that beautiful sanctuary and the many fine people we met there will always have a primary place in my memory treasure chest.

After about two and a half years on my own, I developed a back problem that led me to consider leaving my large house and moving near one of my sons. This I did. Only those who have lived thirty years in one place will understand that it was not easy leaving Chevy Chase and the Washington area, my neighbors and friends, the "Teacuppers," Fourth Presbyterian Church, Chevy Chase Methodist Church, and thirty years of memories. To leave

Gwen and Marie and our thirty years of "Monday mornings together with Jesus" cut deep. I would like to share the June fifteenth entry in one of our favorite devotional books *A Table in the Wilderness* by the great Chinese Christian, Watchman Nee:

> "For where two or three are gathered together in my name, there am I in the midst of them" (Matthew 18:20).

The preceding verse has given a wonderful promise of answered prayer but the promise is conditional. There must be at least two, and they in agreement. Why is their prayer answered? Because these two or three "are gathered together in My name." That is, they do not just meet: they are gathered. We see the difference, for to be gathered is not merely to go of ourselves; it is to be moved by the Spirit of God. And they come, not on their own affairs, but having a single common concern for HIS. It is this that unites them in His Name. And when this is so, Jesus says, 'I am in the midst of them, leading, revealing, enlightening.' Praise God, that is not a promise, it is a statement of fact.

And thus, Gwen, Marie, and I have found it to be.

The deep wound of separation has been assuaged to some extent by the telephone and to a greater extent by my surprise in writing this memoir. Under the Lord's direction, I was comforted knowing I was writing this simple book at His direction and under His leading. It kept me close to Jesus, who promised He would heal my deepest wounds. This book is His. To Him be all the glory.

24

Where Shall I Go?

The Lord had told me it was time to move, and as always, He was right. Now the major decision to be made, as it is for most widows was, Where shall I go? It is a very important choice, and it is inevitably sewn with threads of contrasting emotions coloring the final decision in various ways, like putting together a patchwork quilt. There is the thread of relief from decreased responsibility contrasting with the poignancy and pain in leaving behind cherished family memories. There is the thread of reawakening excitement of change and new stimulation, countered by the tugs at your heartstrings as you ponder leaving behind long cherished friends, neighbors, and church.

Yet the time does come when that very important decision must be made. When my time came, I had one starting point. I would look for a place near, but not with, one or the other of my two sons.

Equipped with a record of my financial assets, I started looking with Richard in his area of North Carolina. As you know, I lean to the South and was quite sure in my heart of hearts we would find just the right house in his area.

After searching and finding nothing suitable in Richard's surrounding area, we drove to Hilton Head Island, where Richard had contacted a real estate agent to show us some property there. I retired that evening in good spirits and a sense of anticipation. Richard retired holding an open mind.

As you know, I had been "branded—in a Biblical sense. "In all your ways acknowledge Him and He will direct your paths" (Proverbs 3:6). I would never forget that verse, so I had, at the start of my home search, asked Jesus to guide me in the final decision. Nevertheless, between you and me, I was quite sure He would guide me southward.

I had not yet fallen asleep when, all of a sudden, a loud thought came into my mind, *No!* I was surprised enough at that, but what followed surprised me even more! Every desire I had to buy a house at Hilton Head for myself left me! I knew it was useless to go with the real estate man; I knew I would not buy there, and had completely lost interest.

Richard, being Richard, took my news in stride, but of course we made the rounds with the agent. He quickly became aware that I was not very interested! (I felt guilty and sent him a note with an apology.) Richard also spoke to him. He was very gracious and said that it was all part of his job.

The Lord had other plans for me. He led me to a beautiful and spectacular condo in New England, near to Bruce and next to Hans, who would make it all possible. It would have been a costly mistake to have moved to Hilton Head at that time, as I can see now. It is true, as the Bible tells us, "For now we see through a glass darkly" (1 Cor. 13:12). Only Jesus has the wisdom to know what is the best for us. And the best for us is always *His* plan for us.

However, I haven't given up asking Him for a home in the south, at least part of the year. I love my beautiful condo in New England, but the half of my benevolent Jekyl and Hyde, the southern half, has the carpet bag packed and ready for at least a six-month stay in my beloved South. God Willing.

25

The Quest Concluded

The Quest has brought me into loving surrender to Jesus. I was not spared suffering, loneliness, and struggle, nor was I carried through life on soft velvet-covered cushions. However, I was holding the hand of someone who knew the meaning of pain and suffering. He assured me that He would never leave me nor forsake me. He reminded me that His strength was made perfect in my weakness. Through it all, He kept me from falling as He continued to shape me into an instrument He could, hopefully, use for His purposes, however humble they may be.

This book is utterly His. The only thing I had to give Him was myself. He took me and is still working to conform me to His image.

It seems fitting that at the end of my book I should go back to its beginning. My Quest was to learn who Jesus was, what He did for me, and to grow into a familiar personal relationship with Him. Throughout the process of living my life, with all its struggles along the way, He has become not only the Savior from my sins but has also given me the gift of eternal life through His life within. He is, as well, my personal friend and confidant. I talk to Him and listen to Him as I write down His thoughts and answers to my questions in my notebook.

Each crisis in my life has brought me into a deeper fellowship with Him. My weaknesses and my needs have become blessings as they brought me closer to Him. My life is still far from reflecting Him, which is my heart's desire. But He is my friend and companion and is patient with me when I often fail Him.

My Quest has brought me to the feet of Jesus Christ of Nazareth. He has proclaimed, "I am the Way, the Truth, and the Life" (John 14:6). To know Him and to make Him known is my divine imperative. To Him be all the Glory!

One final thought: Remember, Jesus has a sense of humor. Love and laugh a little with Him along the way!

Epilogue

Over the years as Gwen, Marie, and I worked in the inner city of Washington, D.C., we became aware of the need, both financial and emotional, of many families in the area, especially those with children but no fathers in the home.

As much as *The Quest* is my personal testimony, it is also a plea to help those mothers who are struggling to raise their children, particularly their sons, alone, in an environment filled with drugs, temptation, and peer pressure. Gwen, Marie, and I experienced the consequences of this environment firsthand when we lost two of the boys in the second family we were given by the caseworker. As recounted in this book, the elder boy died of AIDS and the younger from an overdose of drugs and alcohol. It was not something we read about. It was something we experienced. They were *our* boys and they were *our* friends.

Because of our concern, the three of us have set up a memorial fund in the name of the boys. Anyone wishing to make a contribution to this fund can mail their check to:

The Timothy and Jay Carl Memorial Fund
Central Carolina Bank (CCB)
276 Concord Pkwy., S.
Concord, NC 28207

All proceeds from the fund will be forwarded to the D.C. Department of Human Services to help needy families in the inner city of Washington, D.C.

To order additional copies of

THE QUEST

Call Toll free: (877) 421-READ (7323)

Or write to:

WinePress Publishing
PO Box 428
Enumclaw, WA 98022

The books will be provided at no cost (see Epilogue), but a $5.95 charge* will be necessary to cover shipping and handling.

www.winepresspub.com

Washington residents please add 8.4% tax.
*Add $1.00 S&H for each additional book ordered.